Coleridge

Past Masters

AQUINAS Anthony Kenny
FRANCIS BACON Anthony Quinton
BERKELEY J. O. Urmson
BURKE C. B. Macpherson
CARLYLE A. L. Le Quesne
COLERIDGE Richard Holmes
CONFUCIUS Raymond Dawson
DANTE George Holmes
DARWIN Jonathan Howard
ENGELS Terrell Carver

GALILEO Stillman Drake
HOMER Jasper Griffin
HUME A. J. Ayer
JESUS Humphrey Carpenter
KANT Roger Scruton
MACHIAVELLI Quentin Skinner
MARX Peter Singer
MONTAIGNE Peter Burke
PASCAL Alban Krailsheimer
TOLSTOY Henry Gifford

Forthcoming

ARISTOTLE Jonathan Barnes
AUGUSTINE Henry Chadwick
BACH Denis Arnold
BAYLE Elisabeth Labrousse
BERGSON Leszek Kolakowski
THE BUDDHA Michael Carrithers
JOSEPH BUTLER R. G. Frey
CERVANTES P. E. Russell
CHAUCER George Kane
CLAUSEWITZ Michael Howard
COBBETT Raymond Williams
COPERNICUS Owen Gingerich
DIDEROT Peter France
ERASMUS James McConica
GIBBON J. W. Burrow
GODWIN Alan Ryan
GOETHE T. J. Reed
HEGEL Peter Singer
HERZEN Aileen Kelly
JEFFERSON Jack P. Greene
JOHNSON Pat Rogers

LAMARCK L. J. Jordanova
LINNAEUS W. T. Stearn
LOCKE John Dunn
MENDEL Vitezslav Orel
MILL William Thomas
THOMAS MORE Anthony Kenny
MORRIS Peter Stansky
MUHAMMAD Michael Cook
NEWMAN Owen Chadwick
NEWTON P. M. Rattansi
PETRARCH Nicholas Mann
PLATO R. M. Hare
PROUST Derwent May
RUSKIN George P. Landow
ST PAUL Tom Mills
SHAKESPEARE Germaine Greer
ADAM SMITH A. W. Coats
SOCRATES Bernard Williams

and others

Richard Holmes

COLERIDGE

Oxford   Melbourne   Toronto

OXFORD UNIVERSITY PRESS

1982

Oxford University Press, Walton Street, Oxford OX2 6DP

London Glasgow New York Toronto
Delhi Bombay Calcutta Madras Karachi
Kuala Lumpur Singapore Hong Kong Tokyo
Nairobi Dar es Salaam Cape Town
Melbourne Auckland
and associate companies in
Beirut Berlin Ibadan Mexico City

First published 1982 as an Oxford University Press paperback
and simultaneously in a hardback edition

British Library Cataloguing in Publication Data

Holmes, Richard
Coleridge. – (Past masters)
1. Coleridge, Samuel Taylor – Philosophy
2. Philosophy, English – 19th century – History and criticism
I. Title II. Series 192 B1583
ISBN 0-19-287592-2
ISBN 0-19-287591-4 Pbk

Printed in Great Britain by
Cox & Wyman Ltd, Reading

Preface

Coleridge, the author of *The Rime of the Ancient Mariner*, is one of our greatest Romantic poets: but he is far more than that. He is a thinker and an explorer of the human condition, who once wrote: 'I would compare the Human Soul to a ship's crew cast on an Unknown Island.' His prose work, so much of it broken or unfinished, reaches out all over that island of potential knowledge – into social and political commentary, religious and philosophical speculation, literary criticism and linguistic theory, and not least into the inner world of autobiography, recorded in some 60 private notebooks and nearly 2,000 published letters.

The first object of this short study is to map the entire island of his prose and poetry, and to see Coleridge whole. As a writer and literary personality, he is powerfully of a piece, and for the modern reader his unity, achieved through work and suffering, has a special relevance and attraction. Coleridge is someone who went through a profound physical and spiritual crisis in his middle years. The outward signs of this were a collapsed marriage, a failed career, addiction to drugs, a disastrous love affair, and terrible moments of suicidal despair and sloth. Yet he did not burn out like the other Romantics. He came through alive, sane, matured, still writing poetry and even better prose, still capable of generous emotion, and more than ever influential on his contemporaries. He threw out, said his friend Wordsworth, a series of 'grand central truths'; and he became, in the words of the liberal philosopher John Stuart Mill, one of the 'seminal minds of his generation' who led men to ask of many things, in a new and special way, What is the *meaning* of it? Coleridge earned the authenticity, the authority, of the survivor: the man who, in the Lawrentian phrase, has 'come through'. He speaks to us directly, especially in our anxieties and disarray, of value and meaning in both public and private life, and of what shapes the mystery of our being.

The first part of this book traces the development of Coleridge's career in a personal context, and describes each of his works as it was written. The second part returns to his writings thematically, and tries to disengage certain keywords which provide what may be called the permanent landmarks of his thought, especially in the areas of creative imagination and culture. In doing this I have drawn a good deal on lesser-known works like *The Friend* and the *Lay Sermons*, and while linking these with his poetry, have tried to avoid the conventional emphasis on purely literary discussion. Coleridge is a figure of much broader interest and appeal than that, and in the third and final section I have therefore returned to his greatest poem, the *Mariner*, as a lasting statement of the human dilemma, both Coleridge's and our own – strange and beautiful and questioning, beneath an enigmatic moon.

London
July 1981

Acknowledgements

Acknowledgement is due to the Bollingen Foundation and to the publishers, Routledge & Kegan Paul Ltd. and Princeton University Press, for quotations from *The Notebooks of Samuel Taylor Coleridge* and from the new Bollingen Series edition of *The Collected Works of Samuel Taylor Coleridge*.

My special thanks to the staff of the Highgate Literary and Scientific Institution; of the London Library; and of the British Library. My gratitude to Professor Tom McFarland for several truly Coleridgean evenings at Princeton, which indirectly led to this book; to Ismena Holland for her continuing support; to Peter Janson-Smith; and to Catharine Carver for all her help in shaping the typescript. My most affectionate thanks to Joanna Latimer, of University College Hospital. My greetings to the farmers of the Quantocks who let me sleep in their fields.

This book is for my father, and my mother.

R. H.

Contents

Abbreviations

Coleridge's works quoted in the text are given the following abbreviations, with the relevant volume and page number:

B   *Biographia Literaria*, ed. G. Watson (1965)

C   *On the Constitution of the Church and State*, ed. J. Colmer (1976)

E   *Essays on His Times*, ed. D. V. Erdman (3 vols., 1978)

F   *The Friend*, ed. B. E. Rooke (2 vols., 1969)

L   *Collected Letters of Samuel Taylor Coleridge*, ed. E. L. Griggs (6 vols., 1956–71)

LPR   *Lectures 1795 on Politics and Religion*, ed. L. Patton and P. Mann (1971)

LS   *Lay Sermons*, ed. R. J. White (1972)

N   *The Notebooks of Samuel Taylor Coleridge*, ed. K. Coburn (3 vols., 1957–   )

P   *Coleridge: Poetical Works*, ed. E. H. Coleridge (1912, 1980)

S   *Shakespearean Criticism*, ed. T. M. Raysor (2 vols., 1960)

T   *Table Talk*, ed. H. Morley (1884)

W   *The Complete Works of Samuel Taylor Coleridge*, ed. W. G. T. Shedd (7 vols., 1884)

Bibliographical details of these editions, as of works by other authors referred to in the text, are given in full in the section on Further Reading, p. 98.

1 The writer

I

Samuel Taylor Coleridge was born on 21 October 1772 in the small Devonshire farming village of Ottery St. Mary, on the banks of the river Otter. The glittering water, shining through the green meadows of home, was one of his deepest childhood memories, 'so deep imprest' that long after in manhood when he closed his eyes,

> . . . straight with all their tints thy waters rise,
> Thy crossing plank, thy marge with willows grey,
> And bedded sand that vein'd with various dyes
> Gleam'd through thy bright transparence! . . .

> (P 48)

His father, John Coleridge, was the local vicar: a poor man, a scholar at Cambridge, a writer of school textbooks, and an inspired country preacher. Coleridge was the youngest of ten children, nine of them boys, and clearly the vicar's favourite. Walking home with his father from visits to outlying farms, on winter evenings under the stars, the mystery of the physical universe was unforgettably opened up for him:

> My Father . . . told me the names of the stars – and how Jupiter was a thousand times larger than our world – and that the other twinkling stars were Suns that had worlds rolling round them – & when I came home, he shewed me how they rolled round. I heard him with a profound delight & admiration; but without the least mixture of wonder or incredulity. For from my early reading of Faery Tales, & Genii &c &c – my mind had been habituated *to the Vast* – & I never regarded *my senses* in any way as the criteria of my belief. (L I 354)

John Coleridge had little worldly ambition for his nine sons; only his youngest he destined to be a country parson like him-self, and he used to take him on his knee, and 'hold long conversations' with him. Mrs Coleridge was a personality of a different stamp: practical, highly organised, the driving force behind her children's careers. Brisk and progressive in all matters, she had Coleridge inoculated at the age of three, an event he distinctly remembered, because she tried to blindfold him for the painful operation. But he cried out until 'at last they removed the bandage – and unaffrighted I looked at the lancet & suffered the scratch' (L I 312). He was to do that for the rest of his life.

From the start he was a difficult and unusual boy, spoilt perhaps by his father, demanding of his mother, tempestuous with his elder brothers, inordinately proud of his reading and precocious powers to answer back on any subject. At dame school he moped; at home he quarrelled and went off in sulks to read in the meadows; at night he had bad dreams of 'armies of ugly Things bursting in upon me'. Before the age of eight, he later wrote, 'I was a *character* – sensibility, imagination, vanity, sloth . . .' (L I 348). He had a furious row with his brother Frank over a treat of toasted cheese prepared especially for him by his mother, and flew at the older boy with a kitchen knife. Then he dashed out of the house, and spent the entire night hidden down by the damp banks of the Otter. In the morning he was brought back by a neighbour. 'I remember, & never shall forget, my father's face as he looked upon me while I lay in the servant's arms – so calm, and the tears stealing down his face' (L I 353). Coleridge always regarded this incident as psychologically formative; and it may also have been the cause of a bout of rheumatic fever, which weakened his heart and plagued him with rheumatic pains for the rest of his life, with terrible consequences.

In October 1781, just before his ninth birthday, Coleridge was woken by a shriek from his mother – '& I said, "Papa is dead."' Henceforth his life changed. The following spring he was sent away to London to attend a preparatory school; and moved from there to Christ's Hospital, where he remained as a boarder until 1791, a 'blue-coat' charity scholar. He became a brilliant student of the classics, plunged into Platonic philosophy, dabbled in radical authors, and made many friends, among them Charles Lamb, the future essayist, and Leigh Hunt. Yet during the school holidays Coleridge rarely went back to Ottery

St. Mary (staying mostly with an uncle in London), and he felt cast out from home and family, later writing to his parson brother, the Reverend George Coleridge, in a poem that he was 'too soon transplanted, ere my soul had fix'd / Its first domestic loves; and hence through life / Chasing chance-started friendships . . . ' (P 174) This deep sense of homelessness, and a corresponding search for friendship, and confirmation of his own worth, became one of the abiding impulses of his adult life.

In October 1791, at the age of nineteen, Coleridge went up to Jesus College, Cambridge, on a Christ's Hospital Exhibition, and with a small allowance provided by George. His career as a schoolmaster-clergyman now seemed safely marked out, except that there was a sultry brilliance about his intellect, an extravagance in his behaviour, and a wildness in his letters which suggested otherwise. He drank and grew his hair long, wrote Greek verses 'like a mad dog', bought a swansdown waistcoat, and in his first year won a College medal for a long poem on the slave trade. In his second year he was one of four finalists for the coveted Craven Scholarship. Unduly depressed at his failure to win it, he got ill and into debt, took opium as a pain-killer, and had some acquaintance with Sal Hall, a renowned Cambridge prostitute. He spent much of his vacations with Tom Evans, a friend from Christ's Hospital, and fell in love with Tom's lively sister Mary. Brother George paid his debts, wrote solemn paternal letters, and worried about him.

It was an intensely exciting period for undergraduates. News of the French Revolution, and hope for some millennial change in society, dominated all minds. Coleridge read Edmund Burke's *Reflections on the Revolution in France*, Tom Paine's radical reply *The Rights of Man*, and the anarchist philosopher William Godwin's vision of an ideal egalitarian society, *An Enquiry Concerning Political Justice*. He also read Voltaire, and the materialist philosopher David Hartley, who had propounded in his *Observations on Man, His Frame, His Duty and His Expectations* (1749) that the moral sense was not a divine spark in man, but merely the product of a psychological 'association of ideas', obeying purely physical laws. Coleridge's religious faith was shaken, and a battle of political and moral principles started in his mind, which he was to spend a lifetime analysing and testing. He attended the academic trial, in Cambridge, of William Frend, a tutor at Christ's who was dismissed for writing a subversive Unitarian pamphlet, and was almost arrested himself by the University proctors for clapping and calling out. Then, in December 1793, he suddenly threw everything up, went down to London, got drunk and, without telling friends or family or even Mary Evans, enlisted in the 15th Light Dragoons under the absurd name of Silas Tomkyn Comberbache.

The next two years, 1794–5, were the most hectic and in some ways the most formative of Coleridge's life. After two miserable months in the Dragoons, spent mostly in the stables and the sick bay, his whereabouts were discovered by George, who bailed him out on grounds of 'insanity'. He returned briefly to Cambridge, and then set off on a Welsh walking tour. Calling in at Oxford in June 1794, he first met the poet Robert Southey. Between them they decided to break with all the old political and moral prejudices of unredeemed society, and found an ideal commune in America, on the banks of the river Susquehannah. Six young couples, each contributing capital according to their means, were to share equally in farming, domestic work, building and running the communal estate, and educating the children. Coleridge and Southey went together to Bristol to set up the project, recruit friends, and discover details about sea passages and land purchase.

It was a serious scheme, well researched by Coleridge, who characteristically found a name for it – 'Pantisocracy' from the Greek: a society ruled by all (*pan*) equally. While Pantisocracy was 'easy' as an abstract proposition, he told Southey,

> it requires the most wakeful attentions of the most reflective minds in all moments to bring it into practice – It is not enough, that we have once swallowed it – The *Heart* should have *fed* upon the *truth*, as Insects on a Leaf – till it be tinged with the colour, and shew its food in every the minutest fibre. In the book of Pantisocracy I hope to have comprised all that is good in Godwin. . . . (L I 115)

The striking image, with its strange but precise observation of biological processes in nature, and the moral problem they illustrate (how to convert a truth of the 'head' into a truth of the

'heart' and daily life), are a first sign of Coleridge's most distinctive gift: the combination of poetical and metaphysical insight.

The intense friendship with Southey, while it released Coleridge's intellectual powers, had the effect of dominating him
emotionally: a pattern that was to recur in several later relationships. Southey was engaged to a Bristol girl, Edith Fricker,
and to fit into the scheme for Pantisocratic couples, he hustled
Coleridge into a similar pledge to her younger sister, Sara.
When Coleridge returned to Cambridge for the autumn term of
1794 (reinstated through brother George's diplomacy), his mind
was in a ferment, and he wrote in an explosion of capital letters
and exclamation marks: 'My God! how tumultuous are the
movements of my Heart – Since I quitted this room what and
how important Events have been evolved! America! Southey!
Miss Fricker!' (L I 103).

He now began to write poetry seriously. He revised a school-
boy poem on the young Bristol poet Chatterton, who had committed suicide at the age of seventeen with an overdose of medi-
cinal arsenic and opium. This became the 'Monody on the
Death of Thomas Chatterton', his first experiment with the long
irregular or 'open' ode form. And in December 1794 he
achieved his first publication, with a series of twelve 'Sonnets
on Eminent Characters', which appeared in the columns of the
Morning Chronicle, a leading national daily paper. Each sonnet
praised someone in public life whom Coleridge particularly
admired: revolutionary national leaders like Lafayette and the
Polish general Kosciusko; the writers William Godwin and
Priestley and Edmund Burke, but also the comic dramatist
Sheridan and the mild, conversational sonneteer, the Reverend
William Bowles. Both Southey and the beautiful tragic actress
Mrs Siddons got sonnets; as did Thomas Erskine, the barrister
who had defended four members of the radical London Corre-
sponding Society in the celebrated treason trials of that autumn.

Coleridge's poems attracted considerable attention in the
capital, and he now decided to leave Cambridge without
taking a degree, and go to London. There he lodged at the Cat
and Salutation tavern, and met many leading writers, dined out
with newspaper editors, and renewed his friendship with
Charles Lamb. He much impressed Godwin and his publisher

Joseph Johnson, and a promising career as a free-lance writer opened up. But in February 1795, Southey swept him back to Bristol and the arms of Sara Fricker.

Though plans for the Pantisocracy soon collapsed, the partnership with Southey was immensely stimulating. While they lodged together in College Street, Bristol, during the summer of 1795, Coleridge wrote the lively series of lectures and pamphlets which form his first notable work, the *Lectures 1795 on Politics and Religion*. It includes six 'Lectures on Revealed Religion, Its Corruptions and Its Political Views'; a fine attack on the slave trade; and a popular pamphlet, bringing together much of this material under the title of *Conciones ad Populum: or Addresses to the People*, which attacked the Government and the war against France, yet criticised the extremist elements in the Revolution, and advocated the political and moral education of the English poor and working classes. In the 'Lectures on Revealed Religion', delivered that summer, he fiercely criticised the atheism of many radicals, with its narrow mechanical reasoning, defended the historical truth of the Jesus of the Gospels, and propounded a radical view of Christianity opposed to the accumulation of private property, riches and all forms of commercial empire.

Coleridge's Bristol lectures brought him local notoriety. He was profiled in the newspapers as an uncombed democrat, and barracked by 'patriot' Tory audiences. He reacted coolly, showing his robust good humour – and even a sort of exhibitionism – in adverse circumstances: 'Mobs and Mayors, Blockheads and Brickbats, Placards and Press gangs have leagued in horrible Conspiracy against me . . . Two or three uncouth and unbrained Automata have threatened my Life – and in the last Lecture the Genus infimum were scarcely restrained from attacking the house in which the "damn'd Jacobine was jawing away"' (L I 152).

Among the local democrats, Coleridge soon gained not merely supporters, but close personal friends: a radical-minded Unitarian preacher, John Prior Estlin, who wanted him to join the ministry; the Bristol bookseller and publisher Joseph Cottle, who promised to publish his poetry; two rich Nonconformist brothers, Tom and Josiah Wedgwood, heirs to the Midlands pottery empire. And Tom Poole, a remarkable self-made man, an organiser of working men's political and educational clubs, with a leather-tanning business fifty miles south-west of Bristol at Nether Stowey, who was soon to become Coleridge's 'sheet-anchor'.

Southey had inherited money and wanted to start a Welsh farming project – 'the Mouse of which the Mountain of Panti-socracy was at last safely delivered!' according to Coleridge (L I 165). Inevitably they quarrelled. On 7 October 1795 Coleridge married Sara Fricker at St. Mary Redcliffe – 'poor Chatterton's church' – and settled in a beautiful rose-shrouded cottage at Clevedon, overlooking the Bristol Channel, with a rent of £5 a year. 'Mine Eye gluttonises,' he wrote to Poole. 'The Sea – the distant Islands! – the opposite Coasts! – I shall assuredly write Rhymes – let the nine Muses prevent it, if they can' (L I 160). Six months later, in April 1796, his first slim volume, *Poems on Various Subjects*, was published by Cottle; and in September his first child, David Hartley Coleridge – named after the philosopher – was safely born.

Despite growing financial pressures, and bouts of illness which led him once more to resort to opium, Coleridge now entered an intensely creative period. He wrote and revised a number of longer philosophical poems – 'Religious Musings', 'The Destiny of Nations' – which meditate on problems of religious faith and political commitment; and several simple and moving shorter pieces – 'Lines Written at Shurton Bars', 'The Eolian Harp', 'Reflections on Having Left a Place of Retirement' – in which his love for Sara, and the life they had made together at their 'pretty Cot', form the central dynamic inspiration. These are poems of young married love, rather than romantic longing, something rare in English poetry; they manage to contain in fruitful tension both achieved happiness and underlying anxiety for the future, for a career to be shaped, duty to be done, and – as always in Coleridge – metaphysical problems to be solved. They also show Coleridge developing a most characteristic form, that of the poem as conversation with a particular listener: a poem that is partly a letter, partly an inner meditation, partly a form of prayer.

Yet Coleridge did not consider himself a professional poet,

nor could he afford to. He wanted to make his way in public life as a writer, journalist, scholar, teacher and preacher, and solve the great question of 'Bread & Cheese' for his family. He launched a weekly paper, *The Watchman*, which advanced the radical political and religious views of the *Lectures 1795* and ran for ten issues. He began to study German literature, which he considered far more advanced, both scientifically and philosophically, than either French or English. He made plans to translate Friedrich Schiller (1759–1805), the Romantic poet and dramatist; and to write studies of German natural science, German Romantic theology, and Immanuel Kant (1724–1804), the revolutionary metaphysician. He planned to open a private school 'for 8 young men at 100 guineas each' (L I 209), and also lengthily considered becoming a Unitarian minister – having preached with considerable success in Bristol, Shrewsbury, Birmingham and Derby.

But for all his ambitions to do something large and intellectually daring with his life, Coleridge was disorganised, weak-willed, and easily influenced by others' opinion of him. Moreover, his daily existence was plagued by bills, frequent illness, and deep religious doubts, things that Sara's domestic good sense did not touch. Often he wrote letters 'flighty' with laudanum. Yet the letters themselves are dazzlingly quick, humorous, self-mocking; bubbling with intelligence and self-insight. Here is part of a pen-portrait of himself, unmistakably original in cast and perception, from a letter of 1796 to the radical John Thelwall:

As to me, my face, unless when animated by immediate eloquence, expresses great Sloth, & great, indeed almost ideotic, good nature. 'Tis a mere carcase of a face: fat, flabby, & expressive chiefly of inexpression. . . . As to my shape, 'tis a good shape enough, if measured – but my gait is awkward, & the walk, & the *Whole man* indicates *indolence capable of energies*. I am, & ever have been, a great reader . . . Metaphysics, & Poetry, & 'Facts of mind' – (i.e. Accounts of all the strange phantasms that ever possessed your philosophy-dreamers from Thoth, the Egyptian to Taylor, the English Pagan) are my darling Studies. . . . (L I 259–60)

In December 1796, in response to the urgings of Tom Poole, the Coleridges left Clevedon and moved to a smaller cottage at Nether Stowey, with a garden bordering on Poole's own larger house, on the edge of the Quantock hills. Poole organised a subscription of £40 from Coleridge's friends and admirers, and Coleridge began to lay the foundations of a great scholarly *oeuvre*, meanwhile planning 'to work *very hard* – as Cook, Butler, Scullion, Shoe-cleaner, occasional Nurse, Gardener, Hind, Pig-protector, Chaplain, Secretary, Poet, Reviewer, and omnium-botherum' (L I 266).

Coleridge and Wordsworth first heard of each other's work through the publisher Cottle; and they first met in Bristol in the spring of 1797. Wordsworth, also a Cambridge man, was two years older than Coleridge, but unlike him had no public reputation and was living in seclusion with his sister Dorothy at Racedown in Dorset. The attraction between the two men was slower to emerge, but much deeper than that between Coleridge and Southey. Wordsworth, Coleridge later wrote with a kind of admonishment to Southey, 'is a very great man – the only man, to whom *at all times* & in *all modes of excellence* I feel myself inferior – the only one, I mean, whom I *have yet met with* – for the London Literati appear to me to be very much like little Potatoes' (L I 334). It was an attraction of opposites: Wordsworth tall, taciturn, powerfully self-sufficient; Coleridge fleshy, rumbustious, overflowing with talk and sympathy. But they soon discovered two passions in common: poetry and hill walking.

To begin with Coleridge was the dominant partner, carrying everything before him with his enthusiasm. In June 1797 he walked to Racedown, and stayed for three weeks: Dorothy ever after remembered his arrival, appearing over the crest of the Crewkerne road like a portent: 'he did not keep to the high road, but leapt over a gate and bounded down the pathless field by which he cut off an angle.' By mid-July, he had carried the Wordsworths back triumphantly to Nether Stowey, where through Poole's influence they rented Alfoxden, a large empty house two miles west of the village, perched on the edge of the Quantock hills with superb views of the surrounding woods and coastline. Coleridge also summoned Charles and Mary Lamb down from London. He had, after all, achieved a kind of West Country Pantisocracy.

Throughout the summer and autumn, and into the spring of 1798, Coleridge and Wordsworth wrote and walked together in the Quantocks. Often they composed together, sitting at either end of the large kitchen table at Alfoxden, or rambling for days in the wooded hills and combes above Watchet, Porlock and Lynton. 'Our conversations turned frequently on the two cardinal points of poetry,' recalled Coleridge in the *Biographia Literaria*, 'the power of exciting the sympathy of the reader by a faithful adherence to the truth of nature, and the power of giving the interest of novelty by the modifying colours of imagination' (B 168). Out of these ideas came the plan for a shared book of 'experimental' poems, the *Lyrical Ballads*, with Wordsworth writing about rustic characters and everyday incidents of village life, and Coleridge turning his attention to 'phantasms' of the mind, and supernatural characters and incidents. Coleridge in particular decided to experiment with traditional ballad narratives, with their short four-line stanzas, and hypnotic sing-song rhyme schemes. He began no fewer than four of these ballads between September 1797 and April 1798: *The Rime of the Ancient Mariner, Christabel* (in freely extended stanzas), 'The Three Graves', and 'The Ballad of the Dark Ladie'. Each combines highly picturesque rather Gothick imagery (in the German 'horror-romance' style) with typically acute observations of nature and human psychology. Of the four, only the *Mariner* was ever finished, and first appeared in 1798.

The subject of the *Mariner*, taken from an incident in George Shelvocke's *A Voyage Round the World* (1726), was originally suggested by Wordsworth as specially suitable for Coleridge. It concerned an outcast sailor, mysteriously damned by some primal sin against nature, in the shooting of an albatross in the southern seas. The implications of the story grew rapidly as Coleridge composed the poem, and although he originally thought so little of the work that he intended to sell it separately to Cottle for £5, from the start the persona of the suffering and tormented sailor haunted him, like some emanation of his own unconscious mind.

Yet Coleridge was far from being immersed in his poetic

visions. This was one of the most gregarious periods of his life, and at Nether Stowey during these fruitful months he was visited by many other friends. Among them were Charles Lloyd, a young protégé who subsequently wrote a novel, *Edmumd Oliver*, based on the more fantastic side of Coleridge's character; the publisher Cottle; John Thelwall, who attracted the attentions of a Government spy (as described in the comic 'Spy Nozy' incident in the *Biographia*, chapter X); and seventeen-year-old William Hazlitt, who walked all the way from Shrewsbury, after hearing Coleridge preach and finding himself 'stunned, startled with it, as from deep sleep'. More than twenty years later Hazlitt described Coleridge and Wordsworth in perhaps his finest essay, 'On My First Acquaintance with Poets' (1823). It is full of vivid, living details: Coleridge rushing out bare-headed from the inn at Lynton to enjoy a thunderstorm; Wordsworth quietly and remorselessly slicing up a Cheshire cheese as he discussed the horror-plays of Monk Lewis. Hazlitt constantly contrasts them: 'Coleridge has told me that he himself liked to compose in walking over uneven ground, or breaking through the straggling branches of a copse-wood; whereas Wordsworth always wrote (if he could) walking up and down a straight gravel-walk. . . .'

Coleridge had an intensely energising effect on all those around him, and Sara Coleridge seems to have been happy too: in May 1798 their second child, Berkeley (also named after a philosopher, the Idealist Bishop Berkeley), was born. His friends the Wedgwoods, anxious to help his work and avert the necessity of his tying himself to a Unitarian ministry, generously made over an annuity of £150 for life, at that time a large enough sum to make him independent. Coleridge wrote with unaccustomed solemnity to his brother George that he had abandoned political lecturing, and was devoting himself – 'in poetry, to elevate the imagination & set the affections in right tune by the beauty of the inanimate impregnated, as with a living soul, by the presence of Life – in prose, to the seeking with patience & a slow, very slow mind . . . What our faculties are & what they are capable of becoming. – I love fields & woods & mountains with almost a visionary fondness.' (L I 397)

Stimulated by the Wordsworths and his other friends, he

wrote several more of his conversation poems. They extend the quiet blank-verse form to include not only his domestic loves, and descriptions of the countryside round Stowey, but whole areas of his philosophic thought on the nature of childhood, memory, human conflict, the place of man in the natural world, and the experience of religious transcendence. These poems, not intended for inclusion in the *Lyrical Ballads*, include four remarkable pieces: 'This Lime-Tree Bower My Prison' was written in July 1797, during Lamb's visit, when Coleridge was forced to forgo an evening's ramble through the hills, and sat in his garden brilliantly imagining the course of their walk. Then 'Frost at Midnight', composed in February 1798 while looking after his sleeping child, Hartley, and thinking back on his own childhood. Next, 'Fears in Solitude', written in April after a long walk in the Quantocks during a French invasion scare, with a masterly last verse-paragraph describing his home-ward descent into the nestling village of Stowey with its Palmer-like configuration of church tower and elm trees. And finally 'The Nightingale: A Conversation Poem', composed in April or May during Hazlitt's visit, and as a result of their discussions of the false 'melancholy' use of birds in poetry. It was sent up to Alfoxden with a playful note: 'And like an honest bard, dear Wordsworth, / You'll tell me what you think, my Bird's worth . . .' (L I 406).

The strangest of all his productions at this time, not included in the *Lyrical Ballads* either, and indeed not printed for eigh-teen years, was the 54-line fragment 'Kubla Khan'. It was based on Coleridge's reading from another old travel writer: Samuel Purchas's *Purchas his Pilgrimage* (1617), which describes how: 'In Xanadu did Cublai Can build a stately Palace, . . . and a sumptuous house of pleasure'. The ballad-like opening and clos-ing movements of this famous puzzle-poem – 'In Xanadu did Kubla Khan / A stately pleasure-dome decree . . .', 'A damsel with a dulcimer / In a vision once I saw . . .' (P 297–8) – with its dancing alliteration, and haunting mnemonic childlike quality, suggest that it was originally intended as one of the 'ex-perimental' supernatural narrative poems for the *Lyrical Bal-lads*. But according to Coleridge it was composed 'in a sort of Reverie brought on by two grains of Opium, taken to check a dysentery, at a Farm House between Porlock & Lynton, a quarter of a mile from Culbone Church, in the fall of the year, 1797' (L I 349n.). The poem was a sort of byword in the Wordsworth household; Dorothy christened their favourite water jug or water can – 'Kubla'.

The popular idea of Coleridge in a permanent opium haze at Stowey does not of course fit the facts, even though he wrote to Thelwall that he could sometimes 'much wish, like the Indian Vishnu, to float about along an infinite ocean cradled in the flower of the Lotos, & wake once in a million years for a few minutes – just to know that I was going to sleep a million years more' (L I 350). In reality he was intensely active, finishing a full-length verse drama *Osirio* intended for Sheridan at Drury Lane; constantly book-reviewing; writing nine leading articles for the *Morning Post* on foreign affairs; a long political ode, 'France', about his changing attitude to the Revolution; and a remarkable piece of anti-war propaganda, 'Fire, Famine, Slaughter: a War Eclogue'. His literary reputation grew much faster than Wordsworth's, and he was savagely cartooned by James Gillray (as a libidinous donkey) in the *Anti-Jacobin* – a sure sign of fashionable recognition.

Looking back at that summer 'on Quantock's grassy Hills', Wordsworth remembered it in *The Prelude* (1805) as the magic time 'wherein we first / Together wanton'd in wild Poesy'; but Coleridge remembered it with a very different emphasis in the *Biographia*. His most serious concern had been philosophy, not poetry: indeed continuous, lonely philosophical trial, testing, and self-education as severe as anything undergone by his fictional Mariner:

> I found myself all afloat. Doubts rushed in; broke upon me 'from the fountains of the great deep' and fell 'from the windows of heaven'. The fontal truths of natural religion and the books of Revelation alike contributed to the flood; and it was long ere my ark touched on an Ararat, and rested. . . . I began then to ask myself, what proof I had of the outward existence of any thing? Of this sheet of paper for instance, as a thing in itself, separate from the phenomenon or image in my perception. . . . I became convinced that religion, as both the corner-

stone and the keystone of morality, must have a moral origin; so far at least, that the evidence of its doctrines could not, like the truths of abstract science, be wholly independent of the will. . . . A more thorough revolution in my philosophic principles, and a deeper insight into my own heart, were yet wanting. . . . (B 111–15)

Here was a spiritual – or 'existential' – crisis clearly involving the whole of Coleridge's personality, mind, heart and learning. The poetry was subordinate to this; almost a relief from it – a recreation, in both senses of the word. Yet the poetry drew its sources of power from this deep existential underswell: rather like vivid patterns of foam breaking from an unsettled sea. The prose metaphors of Coleridge's memories of Stowey – the breaking waters, the deep, the flood, and the storm-tossed ark – all connect this inner autobiographical spiritual voyage with the narrative imagery of the *Mariner*.

Once again it was Coleridge who swept the Wordsworths with him, away 'to finish my education in Germany'. They sailed from Yarmouth to Hamburg on 15 September 1798, initially planning a visit of two months. Behind him Coleridge left Sara and his two children in the care of Tom Poole; and the manuscript of the *Lyrical Ballads* (23 poems, beginning with the *Mariner* and closing with Wordsworth's 'Tintern Abbey') in Joseph Cottle's hands for immediate publication – the publisher's advance had been a generous £100.

Germany was a revelation to Coleridge: socially primitive, but intellectually a powerhouse. The two-month visit extended effortlessly to ten, despite all the appeals of Sara. In Hamburg he met Klopstock, and enthused over German wine and the ballads of Gottfried Bürger. November was spent at Ratzeburg, on the edge of the Black Forest, and there the party divided: the Wordsworths went to winter quietly at Goslar, Coleridge took lodgings at the university town of Göttingen. He inscribed himself at the scientific and philosophical lectures; learned German; mixed a good deal into society; attended soirées, danced, drank, climbed the Harz Mountains; and set himself to collect a library of the best German authors, '30 pounds worth of books, chiefly metaphysics – & with a view to the one work, to which

I hope to dedicate in silence the prime of my life' (L I 519).

At Göttingen Coleridge became a European: it was a crucially formative time, opening up his intellectual world in a way that eventually made him the most influential English interpreter of German Romanticism of his generation. He discovered not merely Kant, and the whole notion of an 'experimental method' in metaphysics, making the mind itself the subject of enquiry, but the effect this was having, through the philosopher of aesthetics, Friedrich Schelling (1775–1854), on 'organic' concepts of art and the unconscious; through Schiller on the Romantic drama; and through the brilliant literary critic and poet, August Wilhelm Schlegel (1767–1845), on ideas of poetic and dramatic form. At Göttingen too, a fundamental difference between Coleridge and Wordsworth as writers first becomes clear. While Wordsworth hid himself away at rural Goslar with Dorothy, and began to mine into those memories and inner visions of childhood which form *The Prelude* (first known simply as 'The Poem to Coleridge', his 'friend and guide'), Coleridge laboured, both socially and intellectually, to expand his horizons, and make increasingly large areas of knowledge his province. While Wordsworth dug inwards, solidly and steadily, Coleridge spanned outwards, climbing and traversing on ambitious, perilous scaffolding, exulting at the spreading view.

His stay in Germany was costly in other ways: little Berkeley died in February 1799 – 'I lay the Blame of my Child's Death to my absence – *not intellectually*; but I have a strange sort of sensation, as if while I was present, none could die whom I intensely loved' (L I 490). Understandably a rift opened between him and Sara which chilled both their hearts, and dried up his poetry – 'my poor Muse is quite gone – perhaps, she may return & meet me at Stowey' (L I 493). The Wordsworths, grown homesick, returned to England without him, 'melancholy & hypp'd' because he would not come – Wordsworth himself finally 'affected to tears'.

At last, in July 1799, Coleridge set off for England by a circuitous route over the Brocken. He had large literary plans: a biography of Lessing; a complete verse translation of Schiller's plays; a German travel book based on humorous extracts from his letters; and a definitive general study of Romantic philosophy and metaphysics. He also brought back with him a weird memory of something glimpsed in the Harz Mountains – the Brocken Spectre, a giant figure surrounded by a rainbow of light which was created by the climber's own shadow cast forward on the mists, as he laboured up the solitary steeps, at dawn. It seemed to Coleridge like an emblem of spiritual endeavour, and it came to haunt his later poetry. In the *Aids to Reflection* he was to write: 'The beholder either recognises it as a projected form of his own Being, that moves before him with a Glory round its head, or recoils from it as a Spectre' (P 456 and n.).

II

Coleridge's return to England in 1799, said Hazlitt later, was 'cometary, meteorous, unlike his setting out'. The *Lyrical Ballads* had caused a stir among young writers and critics, the *Mariner* especially being a subject of hot controversy. Major work was confidently expected as the result of Coleridge's German researches. In London he contracted with Longmans to write the travel book, the biography of Lessing, and to do the Schiller translations; he promised Wordsworth to complete *Christabel* and the 'Ballad of the Dark Ladie' for a second edition of the *Lyrical Ballads*; and he agreed with Daniel Stuart, the editor of the *Morning Post*, to write a series of articles on foreign affairs, radical politics, and such leading public figures as Pitt and Napoleon.

Coleridge worked immensely hard: nearly fifty articles appeared in the *Post* between December 1799 and October 1800, and his remarkable translation of Schiller's *Wallenstein* (Part I) was completed in April 1800; he also composed a second part to *Christabel*, though he did not finish the ballad. But the other projects collapsed. Like many young writers (he was now twenty-eight), he had failed to pace himself after his early dazzling success; he was weighed down by over-ambitious commitments, and the expectations of generous admirers like the Wedgwoods and, in a different way, men like Wordsworth, Lamb, Southey and Godwin, who looked on him as a prodigy. His personal life had become unsettled: he had virtually broken with his family at Ottery, he was no longer happy at Stowey (despite the faithful Tom Poole), and he dragged a protesting Sara first to lodgings in London, ánd then in July 1800 to Keswick in the Lake District. Most problematic of all – and perhaps most inevitably, with a man of his quick sympathies and anxious, voluptuous temperament – he had fallen in love again. Not with a literary lady, an actress or a London bluestocking (which might have been manageable), but with an animated and thoroughly likeable Yorkshire girl, a close friend of the Wordsworths, Sara Hutchinson.

This love affair underlay, and to some degree undermined, almost everything he did and wrote in the next ten years. It broke his marriage, it helped to break his health, and it very nearly broke his will to go on with his work. In the person of 'Asra' (Coleridge's code-name for her in the notebooks, usually written in Greek, or sometimes Latin), Sara Hutchinson came to dominate his fantasy life, and greatly increased the sense of personal inadequacy and premature failure, which led to his reliance on opium and alcohol. These traits were already there in Coleridge, the counterpart of his particular genius: in modern jargon he would be called an 'addictive personality', lacking emotional independence in spite of – or perhaps because of – his great intellectual originality. It can be argued that if it had not been Sara Hutchinson, it would have been someone else: Coleridge would have to have had his 'Abyssinian maid', as in the vision of 'Kubla Khan'.

He first met Sara Hutchinson at Sockburn, Durham, in the autumn of 1799. He had gone north with Cottle to see Wordsworth, who was rumoured to be ill and depressed, and to discuss the second edition of the *Lyrical Ballads*. The Wordsworths were staying at the Hutchinsons' farm, and being kindly looked after by the three Hutchinson daughters – Mary, Sara and Joanna. Wordsworth had himself fallen in love with Mary Hutchinson, whom he was to marry in 1802.

Wordsworth had not been able to renew the lease on Alfoxden, but he was still determined to settle wherever he could be close to Coleridge, provided it was in the country and not London. During the course of a recuperative walking tour together in the Lakes, they found Dove Cottage at Grasmere, and the much larger Greta Hall, thirteen miles away at Keswick. Coleridge agreed to move north the following spring, once the Schiller translation was finished: drawn equally by Wordsworth's company and the beauty of the Lake District, which was not unlike a more dramatic and enlarged version of the Quantocks.

His notebooks, previously used largely for memoranda of his reading, lists, addresses and accounts, suddenly explode into life with descriptions of the rivers and mountains, and the subtle effects of light and weather. They also describe (in Latin) how on Sunday 24 November 1799, during an evening of 'Puns & Stories & Laughter' round the fireside at Sockburn, he secretly held Sara Hutchinson's hand and love 'first pricked me with its Dart, poisoned alas! and incurable'. He also adds: 'I did not then know Mary's & William's attachment' (N I No. 1575).

It is clear that Coleridge's awakened feelings for Sara were a third reason for his move northwards, and possibly a decisive one. For besides the new life in his notebooks, his poetry began to flow again. As a result of a visit with her to nearby Sockburn church, with its ancient tower and carved figure of a recumbent knight on a medieval tomb, he began the shortest and in some ways the loveliest of his experimental Gothic ballads, entitled quite simply 'Love'. It is the only other ballad besides the *Mariner* that he actually completed, and he did so with amazing speed and confidence, publishing the finished poem of 24 stanzas in the *Morning Post* of 21 December 1799.

The new series of poems which Coleridge wrote under Sara Hutchinson's influence over the next two years at Keswick includes 'The Keepsake' (summer 1800), 'On Revisiting the Seashore' (summer 1801, after a bathing expedition with Sara to Scarborough); 'To Asra' (1801); 'The Picture; or, The Lover's Resolution' (summer 1802); 'A Day-Dream' (1801–2); and 'Dejection: An Ode', which was first sent as a letter to Sara on 4 April 1802. With the exception of this last, the poems are all more formal and restrained than the conversational poems of the Stowey period: their subject is love, but an increasingly guilty, agonised love, which cannot range freely through the landscape of the poet's mind: which, indeed, has no one to converse with openly, and confidentially. Apart from isolated passages, as when he speaks of love welling up and overflowing through his frame 'like vernal waters springing up through snow' ('To Asra'), Coleridge's own voice seems increasingly lost (P 361).

Where Coleridge is heard now is in the notebooks, and again in many of the letters, which become his primary creative medium. At Keswick he described himself ironically as 'Gentleman-Poet and Philosopher in a mist' (L I 614), but in inviting his friends to join him – Lamb, Godwin, Southey, Poole, the scientist Humphry Davy, the Wedgwoods – he sent the most ravishing, limpid description of the countryside viewed from his study window, and long lazy expeditions across the hills and on the lakes. At the same time, he wrote bitterly and unashamedly to Godwin and Southey about his own failings as a man and a writer; while in a series of letters to William Sotheby, a young dramatist working in London, he brilliantly described his notion of the poet's function, both as an artist and a metaphysician, and of the kind of poetic revolution which he and Wordsworth – in recognisably different ways – were trying to bring about:

> ... a great Poet must be, implicitè if not explicitè, a profound Metaphysician. He may not have it in logical coherence, in his Brain & Tongue; but he must have it by *Tact*: for all sounds, & forms of human nature he must have the *ear* of a wild Arab listening in the silent Desert, the eye of a North American Indian tracing the footsteps of an Enemy upon the Leaves that strew the Forest –; the *Touch* of a Blind Man feeling the face of a darling Child – (L II 810)

Yet all this time, Coleridge's own great writing plans, with the exception of his topical journalism (which continued in fits and starts through 1801–3), were blocked. Apart from the new edition of the *Lyrical Ballads* (containing 'Love', but not *Christabel*), and a reissue of his own *Poems* in 1803, he was to publish nothing in book form for over ten years. Two notebook entries towards the end of 1803 – after the fourth unproductive summer at Greta Hall – vividly exemplify the position, first on a professional, and then on a personal plane. The first opens with a characteristic image from the natural world, almost religious in its intensity, which in better times would have gone into his poetry:

> Slanting Pillars of Light, like Ladders up to Heaven, their base always a field of vivid green Sunshine. – This is Oct. 19. 1803. Wed. Morn. tomorrow my Birth Day, 31 years of age! – O me! my very heart dies! – This *year* has been one painful Dream: I have done nothing! – O for God's sake, let me whip & spur, so that Christmas may not pass without some thing having been done: – at all events to finish The Men & the Times, & to collect them & all my Newspaper Essays into one Volume; to collect all my poems, finishing the Vision of the Maid of Orleans, & the Dark Ladie, & make a second Volume; & to finish Christabel. (N I No. 1577)

But none of this was done.

The second entry, made at the end of the same day, again opens with an observation of nature, continuing that imagery of waters, floodings, and transformations which powerfully connects his poetic with his philosophic voyaging. Even in the private stronghold of his study, he is 'at sea' in every sense:

> . . . the Lake has been a mirror so very clear, that the water became almost invisible – & now it rolls in white Breakers, like a Sea; & the wind snatches up the water, & drifts it like Snow: – and now the Rain Storm pelts against my Study Window! – O Asra Asra why am I not happy! why have I not an unencumbered Heart! these beloved Books still before me, this noble Room, the very centre to which a whole world of beauty converges, the deep reservoir into which all these streams & currents of lovely Forms flow – my own mind so populous, so active, so full of noble schemes, so capable of realising them: this heart so loving, so filled with noble affections – O Asra! wherefore am I not happy! why for years have I not enjoyed one pure & sincere pleasure! – one full Joy! – one genuine Delight, that rings sharp to the Beat of the Finger! – all cracked, & dull with base Alloy. . . . But still have said to the poetic Feeling when it has awak'd in the Heart – Go! – come tomorrow. (N I No. 1577)

Through the painful exclamations and desperate self-analysis of such passages as these, Coleridge's prose itself gathers a new kind of poetic force and authority. The images have a peculiar resonance, that reaches far into the nineteenth century: the 'Beat of the Finger' for example calls up an image from a more deliberate prose poem, Arthur Rimbaud's *Illuminations*: 'Un coup de ton doigt sur le tambour décharge tous les sons et commence la nouvelle harmonie.' That 'new harmony' was partly what Coleridge sought to release. The language of the notebooks, with its fluctuation here between joy and profound spiritual depression, between storm and sterile calm, also moves directly – and almost without transition – into the full poetic language of his masterpiece of this time: 'Dejection: An Ode'.

The question that lies behind, and informs, that poem, especially in the full 340-line version he wrote as an actual letter to Sara Hutchinson, is: What had gone wrong with Coleridge's life? Why, as a writer and as a man, was he becalmed – like the Mariner – in a kind of life-in-death? Why, in the midst of such beauty, and such friendship, was he in hell, utterly alone, his vision lost?

> O dearest Sara! in this heartless Mood
> All this long Eve, so balmy & serene,
> Have I been gazing on the western Sky
> And its peculiar Tint of Yellow Green –
> And still I gaze – & with how blank an eye!
> And those thin Clouds above, in flakes & bars,
> That give away their Motion to the Stars;
> Those Stars, that glide behind them, or between,
> Now sparkling, now bedimm'd, but always seen;
> Yon crescent Moon, as fix'd as if it grew
> In its own cloudless, starless Lake of Blue –
> A boat becalm'd! dear William's Sky Canoe!
> – I see them all, so excellently fair!
> I see, not feel, how beautiful they are.

(L II 791)

It is easy to attribute Coleridge's situation to one cause: opium. But a broad reading of his letters, notebooks and poems of this time – and also Wordsworth's – does not really bear this out. Opium looks much more like a symptom – a recurrent physical retreat from an intolerable position – than a motivating cause. Moreover Coleridge used other 'tranquillising' and analgesic substances as a means of escape and relaxation, notably brandy. The actual causes are far more deep-rooted in his personality. They lay in his intellectual gifts; in the kind of life and creative friendships he wished to maintain (still recognisably inspired by pantisocratic ideals of openness and sharing); and indeed in the historical conditions of the times, with liberalism in retreat, and England isolated from Europe by fourteen years of grinding continental warfare and naval blockade. It was a bad time to be the kind of writer Coleridge wanted to be. For Wordsworth it was bad too: but he had different kinds of resources to fall back on – unshakeable family affections, an inward autobiographical well of poetry sunk deep into his childhood, a stoic single-minded temperament and – from 1802 onwards – a tranquil and fulfilling marriage, made wisely in the maturity of both partners.

Coleridge first published a version of 'Dejection' in the *Morning Post* of 4 October 1802. It was the day of Wordsworth's marriage to Mary Hutchinson, and also the seventh anniversary of his own marriage to Sara Fricker. The poem is about these things too, implicitly in the shortened public version, explicitly in the full manuscript version of the *Letters*. But in the dramatic imagery that sweeps through both – the gathering storm, the great clash of unseen armies, the little child lost on the wild moor – it is about a man spiritually and intellectually isolated in his life and times. It is a lament for an historical fate. Coleridge writes as a European shut away in a remote northern kingdom with his library and his thoughts: tangled in the skeins of metaphysics, depression, opium, sexual fantasy, unwritten books and rain – with nothing but the hope of remote and distant stars, 'Silent, as tho' they *watch'd* the sleeping Earth!' (L II 795).

Both the poetry and the letters of this period also enact a growing debate, and indeed conflict, with Wordsworth over the writer's role. The collaboration of the Stowey days had moved on to a different footing: Coleridge urging Wordsworth to become a philosophical poet; Wordsworth upbraiding, almost punishing Coleridge, for his doubts, uncertainties, questionings, and moral confusion. 'Dejection' is answered in specific terms, and with deliberate echoings of phrase, by Wordsworth's great poem 'Ode on the Intimations of Immortality in Early Childhood.' The two works must be read together. Moreover the power relation, so to speak, between the two men had altered. Wordsworth was now clearly the dominant creative figure, driving ahead with the writing of *The Prelude*, and deciding with crushing finality that *Christabel* was not to be included in the second edition of the *Lyrical Ballads*. At another level, Coleridge was jealous of Wordsworth's sexual happiness, and his creative power. Slowly and painfully (for the attractions of the Grasmere household, especially with the presence of Sara Hutchinson, were never so great), Coleridge realised that he would have to break away from the Lake District – his study at Greta Hall, his marriage, his unfulfilled love affair – if he was ever to develop fully as a writer.

Despite his rheumatic illness, his opium, his drinking, his increasing periods of prostrating depression and sloth, Coleridge remained capable throughout these years of immense and frequently heroic physical exertion. In 1802 he made a celebrated solo ascent of Scafell Pike (the highest point in England), recounted in a superb running letter to Sara Hutchinson; and a wild tour of Wales and Somerset with Tom Poole and the Wedgwoods. In 1803, he embarked on a lone trek through the Scottish Highlands, and covered 263 miles from Fort William via Inverness to Perth, in just eight days.

In the spring of 1804, he decided to abandon everything and go alone to Malta, on a wartime naval convoy. Coleridge was abroad for more than two years, and he cut himself off almost totally from England. His family (he now had three children) had been left at Greta Hall in the care of Robert Southey, and the Wedgwood annuity had been made over to them. His friends received less than a dozen letters in 1804, less than half a dozen in 1805. He gave up all attempts to write, except for his notebooks, which contain a stream of brilliant observations, travel anecdotes, dreams, prayers, nightmares, self-analysis, metaphysical speculations, and isolated passages of poetry – but all utterly fragmented, in a kind of glistening chaos. There was no systematic study as in Germany, no planning of great works. Coleridge was attempting to rebuild his life, recover his health, take stock of his position.

At Malta, Coleridge established himself with considerable success in the wartime Civil Service. The island, with its harbour at Valletta, occupied a key position in British maritime strategy, and its High Commissioner, Sir Alexander Ball, was an ex-admiral with a distinguished naval record. It tells a lot about Coleridge's character that, even at this time of inner doubts and struggles, he made an immediate impression on Ball, who appointed him first as his unofficial private secretary in July 1804; and then his Acting Public Secretary in January 1805. The hot southern Mediterranean climate and the long siestas suited Coleridge: he climbed all over the island, made notes on its sites and monuments, and spent both the autumns of 1804 and 1805 in Sicily, where he twice clambered up Mount Etna. His notebooks show, however, that his opium-taking grew worse, and he was more than ever haunted by thoughts of Asra.

In September 1805, shortly before the battle of Trafalgar, Coleridge resigned from his post, and sailed via Sicily to Naples, where he wintered, moving north to Rome in the spring of 1806. At this point neither his family nor the Wordsworths had the least idea of his whereabouts, and he was rumoured to be lost in North Africa (another odd reminder of Rimbaud). In Rome he was a minor celebrity; he made friends with the American society painter Washington Allston, who executed a striking portrait of him – now in his thirty-fifth year, his face much fatter and coarsened, his hair cut short and going prematurely white at the temples. He dined out with several German scientific and literary men – notably Ludwig Tieck and Wilhelm von Humboldt – and planned to continue his wanderings to Vienna. Tieck's sister wrote in a letter about 'a wonderful Englishman who had studied Kant, Fichte, Schelling, and the old German poets and admired Schlegel's translations of Shakespeare unbelievably'.

But Rome was in the hands of the French, and Coleridge was warned that his connections with the political columns of the *Morning Post* were being traced by the authorities, and he risked arrest as a spy if he lingered. He therefore hurried north to Florence, and then Livorno. There, amid drug-confused adventures and the loss of books, papers and money, he was taken aboard an American ship and arrived at Portsmouth in August 1806, after a terrible crossing of 55 days, during which time he suffered great pain and humiliation from seasickness, constipation and stomach cramps, resulting directly from opium.

Coleridge returned a sick man, but a determined one. His plans were forthright: he would try once again to pursue a professional literary career in London; he would separate formally and legally from his wife; abandon Greta Hall and the Wordsworths; take on enough regular journalism to earn a salary of £400; give a series of lectures on 'Poetry and the Fine Arts' (with material obtained from his gallery visits in Rome and Florence) at the Royal Institute; and set to work once again on his major study of European metaphysics. The Wedgwood annuity would be left with Sara, and his own earnings would help to send Hartley and Derwent, his youngest son, to school – perhaps Christ's Hospital – where they could stay with him in London. He made no immediate attempt to contact the Wordsworths, but wrote instead to his old editor, Daniel Stuart, now running the new *Courier*, a liberal–centre newspaper with a fast-growing readership. 'If I recover a steady tho' imperfect Health,' he told Stuart, he would have no reason to regret his 'long Absence': he had gathered much material in Italy, and he had come to understand how his situation in the Lake District was the source of all his professional difficulties.

For two months Coleridge remained in London, visiting editors and lecture committees, seeing Charles and Mary Lamb, and making a number of influential new friends like Thomas Clarkson, the historian of the slave trade. It was at this time that he collated new stanzas into the *Mariner*, drawn from his observations on his nightmare sea voyage. But soon the Wordsworths swept back into his life: they too were leaving the Lake District, and Coleridge must come at once to join them at Coleorton, on the edge of Charnwood Forest in Leicestershire, where Sir George Beaumont had put at their disposal a large farmhouse. Sara Hutchinson would be part of the household, and Coleridge might bring Hartley with him, and live at Coleorton as long as he liked 'free of all expense but washing'. Wordsworth entreated him 'not on any account to entangle' himself with lectures in London. All this was kindly and well-meaning, but in many ways fatal: once again it undermined Coleridge's struggle for financial and moral independence. After a harrowing meeting at an inn in Kendal, when Wordsworth and Sara Hutchinson remained in Coleridge's rooms from Sunday evening till Wednesday morning, Coleridge was persuaded. He remained with the Wordsworths from December 1806 to June 1807, irresolute and unhappy, at first rejoicing in Asra's proximity, but gradually finding the unfulfilled relationship an exquisite torture, driving him to his notebooks and his opium. He wrote nothing publishable.

Coleridge's submission to Wordsworth has many aspects, both psychological and literary. But it is not simple. Wordsworth still relied deeply on Coleridge's judgement and understanding of his own work; while Coleridge's critical powers were still sharpened and stimulated by Wordsworth's dominant presence. The element of creative collaboration that had brought life to Stowey and Keswick continued in a more painful, difficult way at Coleorton. The highlight of the period was Wordsworth's grand reading of the completed *Prelude* to the assembled household, which produced what is in effect the last of Coleridge's distinctive conversation poems, 'To William Wordsworth', now described as *his* 'comforter and guide' – 'Strong in thyself, and powerful to give strength.' The contrast between the progress of the two writers was further underlined in 1807, by Wordsworth's publication of *Poems in Two Volumes*, the collection that established his reputation. (In fact Longmans offered Coleridge a 100-guinea contract for a similar two-volume collection, but the unfinished *Christabel* deterred him.)

At last in June 1807 Coleridge broke away from Coleorton, and spent a restless summer and autumn in the West Country, staying with friends at Bristol, and revisiting Tom Poole at Stowey. Here he wrote the lovely short lyric, 'Recollections of Love': – 'Eight springs have flown, since last I lay / On seaward Quantock's heathy hills . . .' (P 409). At Bridgwater he first met Thomas De Quincey, another young admirer, who immediately noticed several things about Coleridge: his extraordinary kindness, his never-ending talk, his hopeless procrastination in all practical matters (travel arrangements, letter-writing, dinner engagements), and his magnetic effect on all those around him – even in the high street of Bridgwater he seemed overwhelmed by friends.

By January 1808 Coleridge was back in London, staying in rooms found for him by Stuart, above the *Courier*'s offices off the Strand. Each morning he was wakened by a caged canary, hung at the next-door window, whose fate seemed oddly linked with his own. He had reverted to the original lecture scheme, and between January and June delivered eighteen lectures at the Royal Institute, 'On Poetry and the Principles of Taste', combining literary and art criticism in a highly unusual manner.

His uneven lecture style, sometimes feverish, sometimes dreamy, and his inveterate unpunctuality and postponements (both probably due to opium), were also highly unorthodox. But it was from this time that his reputation as a public lecturer, and brilliant informal speaker at parties and dinners, began to circulate in London. The artistic 'lay preacher' had in fact found a vital new audience, and his professional instinct had been proved right. During the next decade, almost no year went by without Coleridge giving at least one lecture series, either in London or in Bristol. Lecturing is as much a form of theatre as of literature, and Coleridge's increasingly exotic personality, touched with notoriety and marked by his sufferings, proved an irresistible draw. It brought him money, reputation, and some much-needed self-confidence; and though he hated it, he persisted, conscious that it kept alive his ideas as a writer.

In consultation with Stuart, Coleridge spent much of 1808 in elaborating another ambitious plan, which like the lecturing dated back to the early Bristol days. He would launch his second newspaper: 'a literary, moral and political weekly paper', *The Friend*, which was to exclude party politics and topical events, but address itself to the underlying principles that shaped the men and the times. Each issue, printed on quarto sheets, was to consist of a single philosophical essay, with some literary 'Amusement' or poetry attached. Coleridge issued a full prospectus, and eventually obtained 398 subscribers, among

whom were the Foreign Secretary, a number of heads of Oxford
and Cambridge colleges, Walter Scott, Henry Crabb Robinson,
then Foreign Correspondent for *The Times*, and the whole circle
of friends round Wordsworth in the Lakes, Charles Lamb in
London, and Tom Poole in Bristol.

Coleridge had been living with his Quaker friends the Clark-
sons, who had done much to restore his health and limit his
reliance on alcohol and opium. But in the autumn of 1808,
through a series of letters from Sara Hutchinson (who was her-
self ill), the Wordsworths for the last time persuaded Coleridge
to come north, this time to their large house Allen Bank, at
Grasmere, where he remained for the next eighteen months.

Coleridge was able to help Wordsworth with the drafting of
his political pamphlet, *The Convention of Cintra* (1809). But
henceforth *The Friend* had to be written, edited, printed and
distributed from the Lake District, an impracticality that
caused endless delays – especially as the printer lived at Penrith,
which had no coach connection with Grasmere, so that Coleridge had sometimes to walk some thirty miles over the fells to
deliver copy, or oversee proofs. Distribution was also erratic,
and one issue was partly eaten by rats. Wordsworth pronounced
solemnly that the paper would not succeed, though he contributed two remarkable essays, 'On Youth' and 'On Epitaphs',
and allowed Coleridge to print for the first time extracts from
The Prelude. De Quincey, and even Southey at Greta Hall, also
helped; but Coleridge's greatest supporter was Sara Hutchinson. For months she acted as his secretary, amanuensis, subscription clerk, nurse, comforter and cheering companion –
everything except his wife – and if their long, difficult love
affair has one substantial monument, it is *The Friend*.

The Watchman of 1795 had lasted 10 issues; *The Friend*,
an infinitely more ambitious and hazardous enterprise, lasted
no less than 28 issues. After a false start in June 1809, Coleridge achieved the feat of maintaining virtually continuous production for six and a half months, from 7 September 1809
(No. 4) until 15 March 1810 (No. 27), with one special supple-
ment. He said later that 'one main object' of the paper was to
establish in English readers' minds the distinction (which he
drew from Kant) between a narrow, rational 'understanding'

(*Verstand*) and a much broader, comprehending 'reason' (*Vernunft*). As he wrote to one subscriber, the paper required effort and attention, and a continual – almost religious – examination of one's own mental processes: it 'requires the Reader to enter into himself and question his own mind as to the truth of that which I am pressing on his notice' (F II 247).

Early issues concentrated on language, literature, the press, censorship, and the whole notion of communicating truth (No. 3). 'Amusements' included essays on Erasmus, Voltaire, and Luther's vision of the devil (a brilliant analysis of 'objective' and 'subjective' perceptions, in Kant's terminology, in No. 8). The middle issues became more political in character, or 'meta-political' as Coleridge called them: the French Revolutionary concept of government, based on pure reason; the 'Rights of Man' philosophy; Jacobinism and the English 'friends of Liberty' (No. 10) – a series of penetrating critiques. Later issues, obviously written under growing pressure, intersperse moral essays and material provided by Wordsworth and De Quincey with the 'Satyran' letters (based on Coleridge's German travels), and his 'Sketches for a Life of Sir Alexander Ball' (No. 19 onwards). These last, with their glimpses of naval action in America and the West Indies, and anecdotes of Nelson, still fit into the overall schema: they are Coleridge's attempt to define a process of moral education through action – the shaping, in effect, of a philosopher-ruler.

In *The Friend*, Coleridge drew for the first time on the whole range of his previous output and study: political lectures, travel writing, philosophy, historical biography, psychology, polemical journalism and spiritual autobiography. Written and compiled in his thirty-seventh year, and under the most unpromising circumstances, *The Friend* is the first prose work to show not only the quality but the *scope* of his genius. Although much of the original material was inevitably disorganised or obscure, the emergent structure (moving from public to private concerns, from the national to the spiritual) was firm enough to take in much additional and better clarified work in the fully shaped edition of 1818. Constructed like a turret staircase, with its 'landing-places' and spiralling guide rails and steadily widening views, it is another uniquely Coleridgean form: an

education in the form of an anthology, a periodical in the form
of a labyrinth.

Coleridge abruptly stopped writing *The Friend* in March
1810. Subscriptions which were called in after the first 20 issues
(and should have amounted to some £500) failed to materialise;
and Sara, ill and emotionally exhausted, suddenly left Allen
Bank to stay with her brother in Wales. Coleridge, himself
drained and demoralised, with some £200 in debts, drifted first
to Greta Hall to see his children, and then southwards with
Wordsworth's garrulous friend Basil Montagu, who tactlessly
informed him that the Wordsworths considered him an 'absolute nuisance' at Allen Bank, and 'a rotten drunkard'. This
piece of gossip, pathetic in its truth and its triviality, precipi-
tated the inevitable break between Coleridge and Wordsworth
in the autumn of 1810. The two men were never really intimate
again, and Coleridge never returned to the Lake District, except for one flying visit to collect papers from Keswick, when
he drove through Grasmere without stopping. The relationship
with Sara Hutchinson was also over. 'His love for her is no
more than a fanciful dream,' wrote Dorothy briskly and some-
what defensively to Mrs Clarkson. But that is not the evidence
of the notebooks, or the poetry, or *The Friend*.

III

In November 1810, freed but also utterly bereft, Coleridge took
a room at Hudson's Hotel, Covent Garden, and plunged into
opium and journalism. Turned down by Thomas Barnes of *The
Times*, probably because of his liberal politics, Coleridge agreed
to become Stuart's chief writer at the *Courier*, and between
March 1811 and May 1812 he contributed over a hundred leading articles on foreign affairs, the conduct of the war, and social
unrest at home.

In England this was a period of almost revolutionary distur-
bance: Luddism, frame-breaking, food riots, and the assassina-
tion of the Prime Minister Spencer Perceval in the lobby of the
House of Commons, put many radicals of Coleridge's generation on their guard. Coleridge's defence of some Government
wartime policies, and his increasingly virulent attacks on Eng-

lish Jacobins (whom he had criticised even in 1795), made him many enemies. He was attacked in the liberal *Examiner*, and savaged in William Cobbett's *Political Register*; and Hazlitt, now an ascendant power in radical journalism, turned sharply against him with accusations of political betrayal that he was to carry damagingly into his later literary reviewing of Coleridge's work.

But Coleridge's worst enemies were within. His notebooks at this time show him besieged by bouts of terrible depression, hysteria, fits of weeping, hallucinations, long nights of self-laceration and disgust. His betrayal by the Wordsworths, and by Asra; his own betrayal of his gifts and genius; his thraldom to opium: these are his constant themes. Strange horrors and fixations assail him: 'Semen compared with urine is itself a proof and an effect of the natural union of love and lust – thoughts and sensations being so exceedingly – dissimilar from the vehicle – as if a beloved Woman vanishing in our arms should leave a Huge Toad – or worse' (N III No. 4019, Notes). This has a more than literary force of revulsion, an existential horror that recalls the city hallucinations of Baudelaire: as in his poem *'Une Charogne'*, or *'Les Metamorphoses du Vampire'*, where the beloved woman, lying on the bed after love-making, turns into a foul old leather wineskin, *'toute pleine de pus'*.

Other entries in Coleridge's notebooks describe nightmares, monsters, and fearful delusions of disease and mutilation, though it is usually not long before the old genial, enquiring voice breaks in: 'To explain & classify these strange sensations, the organic material Analogons... of Fear, Hope, Rage, Shame, & (strongest of all) Remorse, forms at present the most difficult & at the same time the most interesting Problem of Psychology' (N III No. 4046). From the few poems of this time – 'The Visionary Hope' (1810), 'The Suicide's Argument' (1811), 'Time, Real and Imaginary' (1812) – it is clear that suicide had become a question – though one he did not really answer until 1814.

Yet more than ever, friends gathered round him: Daniel Stuart, the Lambs, Crabb Robinson, Godwin; and most of all John and Mary Morgan, a young family with their own financial troubles with whom Coleridge had long been on terms of intimacy. (Morgan was a friend of Leigh Hunt's, had inherited an ailing tobacco business, and wanted to dedicate himself to literature.) Coleridge was particularly fond of Mary and her sister Charlotte, and described their effect on him as winter sun 'on unthaw' d ice'. To John Morgan, he wrote more freely of his private troubles and humiliations than to anyone at this time. The Morgans were practical people, unshocked by Coleridge's excesses, and many times between 1811 and 1813 they tracked him down to squalid lodgings in the Strand or Southampton Buildings, incoherent with grief or drink or opium depression, and took him back to their house – first to Portland Place, Hammersmith, and later to Berners Street, off Rathbone Place. They also encouraged him to consult a series of doctors – Dr Carlisle in 1810, Dr Tuthill in 1811, Dr Gooch in 1812, and later Dr Daniel – though to none of these medical men did Coleridge yet reveal the true extent of his opium addiction.

Through all this, Coleridge somehow managed to keep working. Between November 1811 and January 1812, he gave a series of fifteen 'Lectures on Shakespeare and Milton' at the London Philosophical Society. The lectures were attended by some 200 people, including even Lord Byron (muffled up in a cloak), and receipts totalled about 300 guineas. Detailed short-hand reports of twelve of them appeared in the *Morning Chronicle* and the *Courier*. Coleridge was uneven, but frequently brilliant, and the lectures were discussed and analysed like a series of theatrical performances. Notably successful were those on Shakespeare's imagination (No. 4); on his wit (No. 6); on his notion of love, especially in *Romeo and Juliet* (No. 7); on his creation of ideal character, as in *The Tempest* (No. 9); on the character of Hamlet (No. 12); and on Milton's Satan (No. 15).

In the ninth lecture, Coleridge referred his audience to a newly published German edition of lectures on Shakespearean drama by Friedrich Schlegel (*Vorlesungen*, vol. II, 1811), which expressed views close to his own. Crabb Robinson, who could read German fluently, noted in his diary that 'Coleridge, I find, did not disdain to borrow observations from Schlegel, tho' the coincidences between the two lecturers are for the greater part coincidences merely.' But throughout the lectures Coleridge employed the kind of broad philosophical and psychological approach to literature which he had learned in Germany, and which was natural to his whole cast of thinking. He reversed the normal categories of criticism then current in England. Instead of dealing with the plays as individual pieces of dramatic construction (to be praised or criticised as a reviewer might), he dealt with them as particular examples of a single creative power. His real subject was Shakespeare's mind, not his plays.

In each lecture Coleridge followed through one feature of that mind at work – the way, for example, it developed styles of speech from a particular, living conception of character – and thus built up a wholly new idea of the creative imagination itself. He also placed Shakespeare in a much wider European frame of reference than was usual, contrasting his Romantic open conception of dramatic form with the closed classical forms of French and Greek drama. Coleridge later modestly said that his purpose in lecturing was 'to keep the audience awake and interested during the delivery, and to leave a *sting* behind – *i.e.* a disposition to study the subject anew, under the light of a new principle' (L IV 924). He did this with formidable effect. The London Philosophical Society lectures of the winter of 1811–12 were the first of a whole series which Coleridge gave in London and Bristol up to 1818, the two volumes of which are now known as his *Shakespearean Criticism*. But Coleridge himself never collected his lecture notes (vol. I), or the shorthand reports (vol. II); and they were never published in book form during his lifetime. However, their influence was widely dispersed (sharpened by the controversy, which continues down to our own time, about how much he owed directly to Schlegel) and their ultimate consequence was a revolution in English criticism.

It is a revolution inconceivable without Coleridge's reading of Kant, as he himself said: 'For Schlegel and myself had both studied deeply and perseverantly the philosophy of Kant, the distinguishing feature of which is to treat every subject in reference to the operation of the mental faculties to which it specially appertains...' (S II 189). Moreover, it produced among his English contemporaries a new wave of Shakespearean study – with Charles Lamb's essays on Shakespeare's plots, Hazlitt's lectures on Shakespeare's characters (1817), and De Quincey's scattered investigations into the psychology of Shakespeare's stagecraft.

Encouraged by his success, Coleridge gave a second set of Shakespearean lectures at Willis's Rooms, in June 1812; and a third set at the Surrey Institute between November 1812 and January 1813. He was also able to give up his regular journalism for the *Courier*, and oversee a bound edition of *The Friend* (published by Gale and Curtis in June 1812) incorporating stylistic revisions and some new footnote material. This was his first book publication for a decade.

But his triumph of the year was theatrical. Supported by John Morgan, who now first acted as his amanuensis, Coleridge largely rewrote his old tragedy of 1797, *Osirio*. Under the new title of *Remorse*, with a romantic setting in Granada during the Spanish Inquisition, the play ran for twenty nights at the Drury Lane Theatre in January 1813. Coleridge received £400 in performance fees and copyright. The financial success was timely, for he had just heard from Josiah Wedgwood that owing to wartime business losses, half the £150 annuity upon which he had relied for so many years was now being withdrawn. Coleridge assigned the remaining £75 to his family at Greta Hall, and wrote a noble letter of thanks to Josiah, making no mention of his own illness or private struggles, and merely remarking that he hoped the play might 'give me heart & spirits (still more necessary than time) to bring into shape the fruits of 20 years Study & observation' (L III 421). He had several projects in mind – an edition of his poems, an expanded edition of *The Friend*, some sort of philosophical apologia for his life, and numerous new lecture series.

As it turned out, 1813 was the darkest and least productive year of his life, which he later described as a 'descent into hell'. There are no letters known between April and the end of September 1813; Coleridge's whereabouts are obscure; his notebooks contain nothing but a few lecture jottings, and desultory thoughts on prayer and religious belief: 'What *comfort* then in the silent eye upraised. *O God! thou knowest!* – O what a Thought! never to be friendless – never to be unintelligible! . . . O feel what the pain is to be utterly *unintelligible* – & then – O

God thou understandest!' (N III No. 4182). It would appear that John Morgan had gone bankrupt, and in August fled to Ireland; the supportive household round Coleridge had temporarily collapsed; he had sunk almost fatally deep into opium. In October he travelled alone to Bristol, to give a lecture series on Shakespeare and education: he mailed money to Mary Morgan and her sister, and found a house for them at Ashley, near Bath. In December, returning on foot through rain and mud to his lodgings at the Greyhound Inn, Bath, he reached the end of his tether and collapsed with fever, and then took near-lethal doses of opium. He was only saved by an old Bristol friend, Josiah Wade, who somehow heard of his plight and brought a gifted doctor, Caleb Parry, to treat him. For the first time his opium addiction was openly admitted to all those round him, and Dr Parry made clear that it was now a simple question of kill or cure.

To Mary Morgan at Ashley, Coleridge wrote on 19 December 1813: 'The Terrors of the Almighty have been around & against me – and tho' driven up and down for seven dreadful Days by restless Pain, like a Leopard in a Den, yet the anguish & remorse of Mind was worse than the pain of the whole Body. – O I have had a new world opened to me, in the infinity of my own Spirit! – Woe be to me, if this last Warning be not taken' (L III 463–4). The warning was taken. Coleridge's experience at the Greyhound, Bath, in some ways represents the nadir of his existence. He emerged spiritually and morally altered, with a much stronger religious faith, a greater humility, and a profound belief that whatever trials and relapses awaited him, he could yet reassert himself and recover something from the wreckage of early hopes. He was forty-one, and on the threshold of a literary rebirth. 'Should I recover I will – no – no may God grant me power to struggle to become *not another* but a *better man*' (L III 463).

After a severe period of medical treatment at Bristol for addiction and suicidal depression (he considered committing himself to a lunatic asylum), Coleridge moved to Ashley with the reunited Morgan family in the summer of 1814. As he slowly recuperated, he began to edit and arrange his poems for a collected edition, the *Sibylline Leaves*, named after the

mysterious priestess of Apollo whose prophecies were said to
be scattered in the dark caves of Cumae near Naples. It was
probably at this time, and in this chastened mood, that he wrote
the prose commentaries which run alongside the definitive
version of the *Mariner*. To the lovely stark verse, in Part IV,
where the Mariner lies 'Alone on a wide wide sea', and looks
upwards in despair and desolation –

> The moving Moon went up the sky,
> And no where did abide:
> Softly she was going up,
> And a star or two beside –

(P 197)

Coleridge now added prose lines which express a whole condition of spiritual exile: man as a part of nature, and yet cut off
from what he alone can perceive as its divine joy:

> In his loneliness and fixedness he yearneth towards the jour-
> neying Moon, and the stars that still sojourn, yet still move
> onward; and every where the blue sky belongs to them, and
> is their appointed rest, and their native country and their own
> natural homes, which they enter unannounced, as lords that
> are certainly expected and yet there is a silent joy at their
> arrival. (P 197)

The growing urge to harvest all his work and study also
showed in a 'preliminary' summary of what he had learned from
Kantian aesthetics. 'On the Principles of Genial Criticism Concerning the Fine Arts' was a series of three short essays, published in a Bristol magazine to accompany an exhibition of
Washington Allston's pictures. Closely following the text of
Kant's *Critique of Judgement* (1790), which argues that aesthetic
pleasure is 'disinterested', Coleridge elegantly distinguishes between common notions of the Picturesque, the Agreeable, the
Good, and the philosophical notion of pure Beauty – a dynamic
balance, he proposes, between two conflicting principles of 'free
life' and 'confining form'.

Allston's exhibition contained a new portrait of Coleridge, executed in this year of recovery: the hair is entirely white now,

almost unearthly against the strict black clothes; the eyes
dreamy and full of suffering, the face fat and pale, but the
mouth retaining its old hint of voluptuous good humour, and
drawn downward with new determination. He might be a radical parson, or a doctor, or an exiled revolutionary.

In the spring of 1815, Coleridge moved with the Morgans to
Calne, a sleepy market town on the borders of Salisbury Plain,
in Wiltshire. Here he began to write a critical Preface to the
Sibylline Leaves, hoping to explain something of the ideas behind his early poetry and the *Lyrical Ballads*; his relations with
Wordsworth; his discovery of German Idealism; and his notion
of the poet as metaphysician. To do this, Coleridge had to combine autobiography, literary criticism and philosophical analysis, in a way that he had never before attempted except in a few
isolated passages in *The Friend*. The result was explosive: the
Preface turned into a two-volume book, written more fluently
and rapidly than anything he had previously attempted. Between June and September 1815, Coleridge drafted all but the
last two chapters of the *Biographia Literaria: Biographical
Sketches of My Literary Life and Opinions*, the book which occu-
pies the central position in his *oeuvre*. Full of his humour, his
erudition, his spiritual anxiety, and his passionate belief in the
imaginative and moral force of poetry, the *Biographia* is one of
the characteristic monuments – the abiding reference points – of
English Romanticism; comparable in its way to Wordsworth's
The Prelude, Keats's letters, Hazlitt's *Spirit of the Age* and De
Quincey's *Confessions of an English Opium Eater*. It is the work
that secures Coleridge in history, and confirms the promise of
the *Mariner*.

As he composed, combining written drafts with dictation to
Morgan, digging back into his notebooks and his memories,
a sense of excitement and release flooded through Coleridge. He
abandoned all attempt at conventional form, and allowed his
'semi-narrative' to sweep freely around three recurrent themes:
his own life-long search for a 'dynamic' philosophy which
would reconcile the truths of nature, mind, and Christian belief; his 'experimental' investigations with Wordsworth into
the nature of the imagination; and his own critical theory
about the workings of Romantic poetry, and most especially

Wordsworth's – which in 'imaginative power' stands 'nearest of all modern writers to Shakespeare and Milton'.

But the overall character of the *Biographia* is that of spiritual autobiography: the voyage and trial of a writer seeking for truth, beauty and salvation; and it is this which links it so closely to the *Mariner*. It is also one of the reasons why it is so extraordinarily magnanimous to Wordsworth, without the least hint of their personal difficulties. Coleridge closes the book in the language of the Romantic theologian, saying that the 'object' and sole defence of his work is the reconciliation of transcendental with rational belief: the assertion that Christianity, 'though not discoverable by human reason, is yet in accordance with it'. He ends with a passage that seems to go back to the very roots of his life and inspiration:

> It is night, sacred night! the upraised eye views only the starry heaven which manifests itself alone: and the outward beholding is fixed on the sparks twinkling in the aweful depth, though suns of other worlds, only to preserve the soul steady and collected in its pure act of inward adoration to the great I AM, and to the filial WORD that re-affirmeth from eternity to eternity, whose choral echo is the universe. (B 289)

This is not only the Ancient Mariner's experience under the blank lonely equatorial night; but also that of the seven-year-old child, trotting confidently beside his father, the parson, in the sweet-smelling childhood fields of Devonshire, gazing up at the starry flock.

IV

Coleridge originally intended to publish the *Biographia* and the *Sibylline Leaves* locally, in Bristol. But in the spring of 1816 he returned to London, and in April joined the household of a young surgeon, Dr James Gillman, at Highgate, where he was to stay for the remaining eighteen years of his life. This was really the harbour that he had sought ever since leaving Grasmere: together the Gillmans – who had fallen under Coleridge's spell at a single meeting – helped him bring his opium-taking under more or less permanent control, and provided the strategic place – poised above London, at a leafy vantage point – from which he could reap the harvest of his career. For Gillman, Coleridge wrote another 'preliminary' commentary on German scientific philosophy, the 'Hints Towards a Theory of Life', closely based on the work of Schelling's two pupils Maass and Henrik Stiffens, and developing 'vitalistic' notions of organic form. John Morgan still acted as his amanuensis and agent, but soon Coleridge was to be surrounded by a new generation of disciples and admirers. It was really a home-coming: he was forty-four.

Publications now appeared in rapid succession, and created for Coleridge a whole new readership, the contemporaries of Keats and Shelley. Lord Byron (then twenty-eight) was the first to intervene, and through his generous influence, the publisher Murray brought out in May 1816 a special collection entitled *Christabel and other Poems* (including for the first time 'Kubla Khan') – a slim volume that was virtually a best-seller, running to three editions by the end of the year. Publication of the *Biographia* and *Sibylline Leaves* followed in July 1817; and a new production of *Remorse* was mounted.

Once he was established at Highgate, Coleridge's interest in current affairs, dormant since the last *Courier* articles, revived in the shape of three 'lay sermons', to be addressed respectively to the Ruling, Middle and Labouring Classes in the form of pamphlets. The first, *The Statesman's Manual: or the Bible the Best Guide to Political Skill and Foresight*, was issued in December 1816, the second in April 1817; but the third – to the 'Labouring Classes' – was abandoned, probably because Coleridge no longer dared to express radical views at a time of rumbling political discontent.

These 'sermons', especially the *Statesman's Manual*, develop valuable concepts of moral responsibility, national education and the 'organic' nature of society; but they are obscure and difficult in style, and superficially reactionary in their topical comment, showing little apparent appreciation of the growing agitation for Parliamentary reform and social legislation. They suggest that Coleridge's private sufferings had shut him off from immediate political realities. But the following year, in April 1818, he published two impassioned 'circulars' (and an open letter in the *Courier*, signed 'Plato') in defence of Sir Robert Peel's Bill to regulate the terrible working hours and conditions of cotton factory children, which had been held up in the House of Lords. The question, as Coleridge bitterly remarked to Crabb Robinson, was 'Whether some half score of rich Capitalists are to be prevented from suborning Suicide and perpetrating Infanticide and Soul-murder' (L IV 854): the characteristic Coleridgean word here is not 'Capitalist' but 'Soul-murder'.

Coleridge was now much in demand as a literary celebrity. He was offered the General Editorship of the *Encyclopaedia Metropolitana*, at a salary of £500 per annum; and a contributing editorship on the prestigious new *Blackwood's Magazine*. These finally came to nothing, largely because of Coleridge's refusal to move from Highgate, but for the *Encyclopaedia* he wrote a magnificent Introduction or 'Treatise on Method'. The other constant demand in 1818–19 was, naturally enough, for him to give public lectures; and he gave many, both single appearances and fully-planned courses. One address for the London Philosophical Society was on 'The Growth of the Individual Mind' – a subject foreshadowing the subtitle of Wordsworth's *The Prelude*. Between December 1818 and March 1819 Coleridge gave a complete course on 'The History of Philosophy'; the notes for this have been recently published, but they say astonishingly little about Kant or Schelling. He also gave a last series of his Shakespearean lectures.

Undoubtedly the most valuable of these late lectures is the 'General Course on Literature', a series of fourteen given between January and March 1818, of which a shorthand report was published in the *Literary Remains* (1836). These show Coleridge at full stretch, ranging brilliantly over early English and German ballads; Chaucer and Spenser and Shakespeare; Cervantes, Rabelais and Dante; Donne and Milton; and such quintessentially Coleridgean topics as witches, mythologies, the *Arabian Nights*, apparitions, *Robinson Crusoe*, nightmares, and the role of the imagination in the education of young children. The lectures are full of his wit and idiosyncratic learning, and constantly enlivened by his twinkling asides that seem to make veiled reference to his own experiences: 'The Robinson Crusoe is like the vision of a happy night-mare, such as a denizen of Elysium might be supposed to have from a little excess in his nectar and ambrosia supper' (W IV 316).

At the end of 1818, Coleridge published the revised and augmented edition of *The Friend*, now a substantial work in three volumes, dedicated to the Gillmans. This really marks the last of his major productions as a writer, based on everything he wished to salvage from his journalism, pamphlets and essays. Volume III of the set, 'On the Grounds of Morals and Religion, and the Discipline of the Mind', was largely new – consisting of a preliminary discussion of the nature of conscience, genius, belief, ethics and morality, followed by the 'Method' of 1818. This last is a *tour de force*, ranging with dazzling virtuosity through the realms of human knowledge (by way of *Hamlet*, coordinate geometry, Plato, botanical classification, Newton, Kepler, magnetism, natural theology, skeletal structures in birds, trade patterns, and the Royal Observatory) in search of a common and universal principle of 'self-organizing purpose' (or method) to be found in nature, man, and all true science: the 'principle of unity with progression . . . progressive transition without breach of continuity' (F I 476). Here Coleridge developed and displayed one of the most influential of his metaphysical or analytic ideas, drawn from Kant's theory of knowledge, and Schelling's *Naturphilosophie*: the notion of 'organic unity'. *The Friend* of 1818 thus forms a not unfitting crown to his active career as a writer.

Coleridge himself felt anything but crowned: to him, everything still remained to be done. Writing from Highgate in 1819 to a friend, he surveyed his output with a modesty which would have checked even his severest critics: '. . . were it in my power, my works should be confined to the second volume of my "Literary Life" [the *Biographia*], the Essays of the third volume of the 'Friend' . . . with about fifty or sixty pages from the former two volumes, and some half-dozen of my poems' (L IV 925). It was not the *magnum opus* he had planned, and still planned in the shape of a philosophical *summa* – the *Opus Maximum* – to be dictated to his new amanuensis J. H. Green (a brilliant young linguist and medical demonstrator from Guy's Hospital, who eventually became the first Professor of Surgery

at King's College, London, and one of Keats's medical super-
visors – typical of the talent Coleridge now attracted).

The remaining decade or so of his life was to be important
largely for his personal influence on other younger writers, his
Thursday evening classes, his unquenchable monologues (partly
recorded in the *Table Talk*, edited by his nephew Henry Coleridge) and his looming presence, a giant of former days, as the
renowned 'Sage of Highgate'. Thomas Carlyle, one of the many
who made a special journey to see him, wrote of him sitting 'on
the brow of Highgate Hill, . . . looking down on London and its
smoke-tumult, like a sage escaped from the inanity of life's bat-
tles'. And Shelley, drawn irresistibly to Coleridge's image, even
in distant Italy, projected him as an almost apocalyptic figure
amidst the confusion of the times: 'a mind, / Which, with its
own internal lightning blind, / Flags wearily through darkness
and despair – / A cloud-encircled meteor of the air, / A hooded
eagle among blinking owls.'

But the most living glimpse of the Sage in full conversational
flow came from John Keats, who met him with J. H. Green one
afternoon in 1819 on the edge of Hampstead Heath, and wrote
breathlessly to his brother George:

> I walked with him at his alderman-after-dinner pace for near
> two miles I suppose. In those two miles he broached a
> thousand things – let me see if I can give you a list: – Nigh-
> tingales, Poetry – on Poetical sensation – Metaphysics – Differ-
> ent genera and species of Dreams – Nightmare – a dream
> accompanied by a sense of touch – single and double
> touch – a dream related – First and second consciousness – the
> difference explained between will and Volition – so many
> metaphysicians from a want of smoking [*sic*] the second
> consciousness – Monsters – the Kraken – Mermaids – Southey
> believes in them – Southey's belief too much diluted – a Ghost
> story – Good morning. I heard his voice as he came towards
> me – I heard it as he moved away – I have heard it all the
> interval – if it may be called so.

Within a fortnight of this letter, Keats had written his 'Ode to a
Nightingale'; and perhaps even more significantly, started his
'Belle Dame Sans Merci', which uses the theme of a lovelorn

medieval knight very closely related in style and atmosphere to Coleridge's ballad 'Love'. Many other writers subsequently made the pilgrimage to Highgate, from Ralph Waldo Emerson to Harriet Martineau, the feminist and economic reformer. Henry James relates a shrewd but purely imaginary meeting in his story 'The Coxon Fund' (1894).

Coleridge wrote an enormous number of letters, on subjects ranging from the poetry of William Blake to the theology of the Trinity, and planned various monumental studies besides the *Opus Maximum*: a three-volume work on Shakespeare; a two-volume history of English and European literature; a technical work on logic; and a collection of letters on the Old and New Testament. But he lacked the health and single-mindedness to organise or complete any of these, and a chaotic mass of papers was left after his death to be published as best they could by his helpers and admirers.

Coleridge felt easiest in the role of educator and spiritual adviser, and as a result of his Thursday classes, he did publish in 1824 the *Aids to Reflection*, a large and unsystematic collection of commentaries and meditations on the writings of the Anglican divine, Archbishop Leighton (1611–84). The work, in which he stressed the importance of Christianity as a 'personal revelation', independent of doctrine and with strong social implications, had a powerful influence on the development of the Broad Church movement, and the reforming zeal of the Christian Socialists – John Sterling, Julius Hare, F. D. Maurice and – for a time – Charles Kingsley.

In his last years Coleridge renewed many personal friendships. He was visited constantly by Charles Lamb (who dedicated his *Essays* to him), Crabb Robinson and William Sotheby. Tom Poole came up from Somerset, George Coleridge from Devon, and Mrs Coleridge and his daughter Sara from the Lake District; in 1828 he even went on a short tour with Wordsworth and his daughter Dora to Germany, where they had a cordial meeting with Friedrich Schlegel. Several times he met Sara Hutchinson in London at social gatherings. His deepest personal sadness was his son Hartley, who was dismissed from his Fellowship at Oxford for drinking, and buried himself away as the village schoolmaster at Ambleside, where he married a farmer's daughter, wrote a handful of beautiful sonnets, and sank into opium addiction.

Coleridge wrote a few late poems, which bear witness to a profound sense of doubt about his own inner worth, and a continual anxious questioning of man's spiritual place in the scheme of things. Most can be only tentatively dated from his notebooks, except for the moving sonnet 'Work Without Hope', specifically assigned to 21 February 1825. This was the day which Coleridge always associated with a 'heart-wringing' letter from Sara Hutchinson, twenty-two years before. (The reference to 'amaranths', the immortal flowers of Elysium and fame, also contains a personal acknowledgement to Hazlitt, who had used the image in his essay on Coleridge, lamenting his lost literary achievements, in *The Spirit of the Age*.)

> All Nature seems at work. Slugs leave their lair –
> The bees are stirring – birds are on the wing –
> And Winter slumbering in the open air,
> Wears on his smiling face a dream of Spring!
> And I the while, the sole unbusy thing,
> Nor honey make, nor pair, nor build, nor sing.
>
> Yet well I ken the banks where amaranths blow,
> Have traced the fount whence streams of nectar flow.
> Bloom, O ye amaranths! bloom for whom ye may,
> For me ye bloom not! Glide, rich streams, away!
> With lips unbrightened, wreathless brow, I stroll:
> And would you learn the spells that drowse my soul?
> Work without Hope draws nectar in a sieve,
> And Hope without an object cannot live.

> (P 447)

Other poems which explore this mood of melancholy and philosophic doubt include 'Limbo' (?1818), in which an old blind man in a garden stands with his face turned upwards towards an unseen moon; 'Constancy to an Ideal Object' (?1826), which returns to the ambivalent, taunting image of the Brocken Spectre; 'Phantom or Fact: A Dialogue' (?1830); 'Coeli Enarrant' (?1830), a terrifying vision of blank, unmeaning stars; and 'Love's Apparition' (?1833). It is notable how often all these touch on the lost spells of 'Kubla Khan', or the remembered night sky of the *Mariner*.

In 1830 Coleridge published his last work, a monograph *On the Constitution of the Church and State*, which can really be considered as his final 'lay sermon'. Its immediate occasion was the national debate surrounding the Bills for Catholic Emancipation (1829) and for Parliamentary Reform (1832). But Coleridge used this as an opportunity to expound the 'organic' and dynamic nature of society, balancing certain principles of permanency and progression, and depending equally on a harmony between national 'civilisation' and individual 'culture'. These politico-theological ideas are obvious extensions of the polarities in his earlier philosophical and literary thought – the principles of 'free life' and 'confined form' – and served to place him influentially in the line of Romantic conservative thinkers about English society: Edmund Burke, Thomas Carlyle, Matthew Arnold, Cardinal Newman. But that he should also have inspired the Christian Socialists (and never quite ceased being a Pantisocrat, looking for his magic river) suggests that in reality his lay sermons contained very little specifically *political* doctrine. What they did was to make readers of every persuasion acutely aware of the shortcomings, the doubts, the underlying spiritual needs of society – particularly as it became more industrialised, more dependent on commercial and utilitarian relations, more competitive and brutally materialistic. In this sense their central function was still imaginative: to prevent 'Soul-murder'.

Coleridge was only fifty-eight when the second, definitive edition of *Church and State* was published, but he already seemed like a frail and elderly man. He had made a will, appointing J. H. Green as his literary executor, and leaving his tiny personal estate in trust to his wife and family. According to the eighteenth-century custom, he also left 'small, plain gold mourning rings' to those that had been closest to his heart – Charles Lamb, Tom Poole, Josiah Wade and Sara Hutchinson. (John Morgan, who would otherwise surely have been included, was already dead.) In a late codicil he also tried to make a special provision for Hartley. Coleridge died shortly after dawn on 25 July 1834, as the result of a heart attack. He was calm and brave in his last hours, gracefully accepting medical doses of arrowmint and laudanum: 'I could almost be witty,' he remarked thoughtfully.

Charles Lamb wrote: 'It seemed to me that he long had been on the confines of the next world, – that he had a *hunger for eternity*. . . .' Wordsworth had his last sonorous word in verse: 'Nor has the rolling year twice measured, / From sign to sign, its steadfast course, / Since every mortal power of Coleridge / Was frozen at its marvellous source.' But the image of the frozen source also comes from Coleridge's own writing, in one of those radiant moments when the poet, the metaphysician, and the theologian of Hope are one. The frozen source, says Coleridge in *The Friend*, is marvellous because it will unfreeze in due season and run on:

> Truth considered in itself and in the effects natural to it, may be conceived as a gentle spring or water-source, warm from the genial earth, and breathing up into the snow drift that is piled over and around its outlet. It turns the obstacle into its own form and character, and as it makes its way increases its stream. And should it be arrested in its course by a chilling season, it suffers delay, not loss, and waits only for a change in the wind to awaken and again roll onwards. (F I 65)

2 The thinker

Qualities of Coleridgean truth

'To awaken and again roll onwards': that is not the end of Coleridge, but only the beginning. Here is a river again, but it is not the river Otter of his birthplace: it is the whole river of his mind and thought. It leads us to his permanent concerns and qualities: the things that make Coleridge not just a figure winding through an historical lanscape, but a close and continuing presence – our contemporary. 'Truth . . . may be conceived as . . . a water-source.' Why is this passage so typical of Coleridge as a thinker? The writing is not exceptionally fine, but the thought is memorable, and it makes three absolutely charateristic demands on the reader. These demands express Coleridge's three leading qualities.

First of all, the passage approaches us imaginatively. It asks us to re-create in our minds the action of the spring, first 'breathing up' into the snow, then slowed and frozen by the 'chilling season', then released again and rolling on. Only by picturing and re-enacting this natural process can we understand what Coleridge has to say about the way truth works. The language is metaphorical, not abstract. Coleridge promotes his argument by making it come alive for us, figuratively and imaginatively. Even in his prose, he thinks like a poet.

Secondly, the passage makes us look at the world dialectically. Coleridge shows one principle or fact of nature (the spring water) in contention with an opposed one (the freezing snow). The water and the snow are in dynamic opposition, working against each other's nature and tendency: the water trying to flow, the snow trying to freeze. This process of dynamic opposition is a dialectical one; and truth, says Coleridge, works like nature – dialectically. Moreover the result of this opposition is not a victory for one side or the other, but a kind of active reconciliation. The water changes into ice, and then the snow and ice change back into water: 'it turns the obstacle into its own form'. They flow on together, combined and mutually in-creased – the flow of truth 'increases its stream'. So the dialec-tical process in things leads to a synthesis: a reconciliation in a more powerful state, or higher reality.

Thirdly, the passage carries a distinct emotional charge: it asks us to consider the mysterious workings of our own heart, and the glorious life-giving quality of the truth that flows out of it – 'warm', 'genial', with irresistible power to 'awaken', like springtime itself. This is not merely a poetic observation of na-ture, or a philosophic argument about mind. It is a celebration of the mystery of our own being: the way truth (and by implica-tion, love) flows out – is checked by doubt, by difficulty, by anxi-ety, by opposition, by trial, by suffering – and then flows on again, enhanced. It is exactly that central experience celebrated in Part IV of the *Mariner*, in the same imagery but with a great-er intensity, when, at the beauty of the sea beasts, the Mariner feels a 'spring of love gush' from his heart, 'and I blessed them unaware' (P 193). So Coleridge is seeking to express a mystical quality at the heart of experience: something that is common to us all, but beyond common reason or common language.

These three qualities distinguish Coleridge's writing as a whole, and shape his entire work and thought, in whatever field. Wherever we look, wherever we track him, we will even-tually come back to these three fundamental considerations about what he has to say to us. It is imaginative, dialectical, and mystical.

I

The role and function of the imagination is so pervasive in Col-eridge that critics have sometimes referred to his 'doctrine of the Imagination'. The very weight that the word still carries in English is largely due to him. In his lectures he frequently stated that the highest faculty in man is not reason or logic but imagination, which provides 'the seeds of all moral and scien-tific improvement' (W IV 318). The universe itself, according to Coleridge, cannot finally be perceived by us either as a mechanical or even a rational construct: only as an imagina-tive one. He wrote in the pivotal chapter XIII of the *Biographia*:

'The primary imagination I hold to be the living power and prime agent of all human perception, and as a repetition in the finite mind of the eternal act of creation in the infinite I AM.' We create – or re-create – the world through our imagination in the same sense that God, the 'infinite I AM', originally created and continues to create it. The imagination of the poet, the 'secondary' imagination, is a special, shaped and conscious form of this primary act 'differing only in degree, and the mode of its operation'. The poet's imagination 'dissolves, diffuses, dissipates, in order to re-create; or where this process is rendered impossible, yet still, at all events, it struggles to idealise and to unify. It is essentially *vital*, even as all objects (as objects) are essentially fixed and dead.' (B 167) The imagination brings life to a dead world.

Both Coleridge's poetry and his prose are a consistent attempt to apply this primordial recognition to a wide range of human phenomena. Whether he is discussing the political implications of Jacobinism; the moral qualities of Wordsworth's poetry; Shakespeare's creation of dramatic character; the role of education in a dynamic society; or the nature of visionary or hallucinatory experience – his first appeal is always to the reader's imagination. To understand such-and-such a thing, says Coleridge in effect, you must make it *come alive* in your mind – you must *imagine* it for yourself. Shelley, who was deeply influenced by the *Biographia*, expressed this memorably in his *Defence of Poetry*, where he observed that our greatest weakness as modern Western 'civilised' people was that we lacked 'the creative faculty to imagine that which we know'.

Coleridge's own imagination belongs to a distinct literary tradition: it is deeply English, rural, and with a strong idealising or neo-Platonic strain. His characteristic imagery is drawn from sun, moon and stars; from rivers, streams, lakes, waterfalls, rain and clouds; from winds, storms, snow; from seasonal growth and change; from birds, insects; from cottage life, firelight, vegetable gardening, church-going; from sea, foam, ships, harbours, sunsets. It is recognisably the same world as that of Turner and Samuel Palmer. Everywhere it seeks the 'radiance' of the eternal in the particular: the 'transparency' of a green leaf in sunlight, or the shining of reflected stars through water.

But there are other important elements. One is the Gothic 'magical' strain, drawn from his reading of romance literature, folk ballads, travel books and oriental tales. Another is scientific, drawn especially from the natural processes to be found in biological life, chemical combination, and the new physics of magnetism and electricity. He wrote with equal naturalness in 1797 of Dorothy Wordsworth's sensibility responding to life like 'a perfect electrometer'; or, in 1814, of Raphael's painting being 'volatilised' and interpenetrated by 'electrical flashes'. His whole notion of 'organic unity' within a work of art, or a social structure, is dependent on such scientific analogies.

The scintillating and original combination of these elements is what gives Coleridge's imagination its characteristic power and range. Though comparable at certain moments to that of Wordsworth or Keats, and in its scientific aspects to that of Shelley, it is much broader than theirs; and though rarely quite so intense, it touches us at a greater number of living points. It is the product of an altogether more deeply educated mind, more universal in its concerns and cross-references from one area of knowledge to another. It is, in a word, more modern.

It is also more anxious. The rich multi-level quality of Coleridge's imagination was obviously achieved at tremendous cost. It contains terrible tensions and contradictions. The struggle between religious belief and despair; between acquired knowledge and achieved work; between a safe, sheltered 'poet's' life (like Wordsworth's) and an active, public, 'professional' writer's life, engaging in politics, criticism, and philosophical teaching (the model for which barely existed in the England of Coleridge's day – or even yet of our own): these are some of the obvious tensions. They are poignantly expressed in his shuttling between London and the provinces; between a domestic marriage and a professional, working partnership; between the laudanum decanter and the lecture hall.

But Coleridge's mind – the sheer capacity of his imagination – took him into deeper historical waters too. Ever after his visit to Germany in 1798–9, Coleridge felt the pull of Europe, the attraction of a larger intellectual community. He recognised that in the very richness and particularity of the English mind; its damp, loamy, empirical grasp of fact and locality; its humorous disputes and studiedly eccentric personalities, there was something narrow and opaque – something that shut out the larger questions, the vast drafty perspectives of philosophic theory and ultimate knowledge. (His passion for hill climbing, whether in the Harz Mountains or on Scafell Pike, is curiously symbolic of this intellectual claustrophobia.) Yet he was cut off from Europe: by a continental war, by lack of money, by the misunderstanding of many friends and critics, who could not really appreciate what he was trying to do with his translations and adaptations from the German; with his 'philosophical' criticism of Shakespeare and Wordsworth; and his life-long passion for metaphysics. They did not see that Coleridge was trying to import, to naturalise, to transplant, something of that wider European mind, that lived so vividly in his own imagination.

II

It is Coleridge's prevailing impulse to analyse and organise the materials of the imagination into *a system*, which most clearly distinguishes him from his contemporaries in England. If one compares his critical writing, even in its most fragmentary form, with the occasional nature of the essays of Hazlitt, Lamb or De Quincey, or the purely intuitive, glancing, improvisatory nature of the literary letters of Keats or Byron, the difference immediately becomes apparent. (And where there is a hint of some larger system, as Keats on 'Negative Capability', or Shelley on the 'moral imagination', the source or inspiration can frequently be traced to Coleridge himself.) By temperament and training he is a system-builder, who seeks to establish a philosophical structure within every experience and branch of knowledge: even when he suffers a ghastly nightmare, or the horrors of opium withdrawal, he tries to fit it into the rules of experimental psychology. The very conception of such works as *The Friend* or the *Biographia* depends upon the search for a philosophical system. He sometimes conceived of his whole work including his poetry as an attempt to reconcile the 'mechanico-corpuscular' system of eighteenth-century English thought with the 'dynamic' and 'organic' philosophy of Kant and Schelling. 'My system,' he told his nephew, 'if I may venture to give it so fine a name, is the only attempt I know ever made to reduce all knowledges into harmony. It opposes no other system, but shows what was true in each; and how that which was true in the particular, in each of them became error, *because* it was only half the truth.' (T 136) J. S. Mill later considered this idea of reconciling 'the noisy conflict of half-truths' one of Coleridge's greatest contributions to progressive thought in England.

The essential terms of Coleridge's reconciling system are dialectical. They stem initially from his awareness of contradictions within his own experience, and especially as a young man in the 1790s – at Cambridge and in the West Country – of religious contradiction: between the psychological and materialist theories of Hartley's 'associationism', which led at best to a kind of pantheism; and the traditional Anglican beliefs upheld by his father. Or more harshly, between radical disbelief and traditional faith: the one pressing upon Coleridge's 'intellect', the other – as he says in chapter X of the *Biographia* – still clinging to his 'heart'. But it was only when he read Kant's *Critique of Pure Reason* that Coleridge found this expressed in a philosophic and systematic way, as the fundamental encroachment of the *subject* upon the *object* in human experience. In the *Aids to Reflection* he urged, as the greatest assistance to clear thinking, the re-introduction into English of 'subjective' and 'objective' reality – terms which are now in completely current use.

Coleridge never set out his system in a single work, but he expressed it most clearly through a series of paired terms of dialectical definition. To his central idea of the *imagination*, he added the balancing (and largely critical) term *fancy*. Fancy does not enter creatively into an idea or object, but plays with them as 'counters', dealing with the world as a set of 'fixities and definites'. In poetry, fancy produces similes and comparisons, rather than metaphors; in discursive prose, it is logical and cumulative. It is really a 'mode of memory' modified by the conscious selecting powers of the mind; 'it must receive all its materials ready made from the law of association' (B 167). This last term clearly links it with Hartleyian, rather than Kantian, concepts of the mind. One of the great differences, for Coleridge, between eighteenth-century and Romantic poetry was that the former was fanciful, the latter imaginative. Coleridge discussed Imagination and Fancy most fully in his letters to Sotheby of 1802; and in chapter XIII of the *Biographia*.

Following Kant, Coleridge also distinguished more generally between the large, embracing mode of *reason*, and the narrower mechanical operation of the *understanding*. This distinction is really based on Kantian epistemology, or the theory of how we come to have knowledge of anything at all outside ourselves. Coleridge discusses it in the final essays in *The Friend*, vol. I; and in a valuable Appendix C to the *Statesman's Manual*.

We use reason wherever our whole personality – intelligence, 'moral being', past experience, and 'conscious self-knowledge' – is brought to bear upon a question. We use understanding more commonly and frequently, in dealing with practical and logical forms, '*real* objects, the materials of *substantial* knowledge', and when we 'generalise and arrange the phenomena of perception' (F I 156). Reason is therefore distinct from 'reasoning', or 'rationalizing' in its usual sense (which belongs to understanding). The great value of this distinction came for Coleridge when dealing with complex concepts like revolution, society, education or belief, where a narrower 'rational' account – however logical and superficially attractive or convincing – does not really do justice to the human imponderables involved. On occasions this also opened him to the charge of 'German mysticism' from radical and utilitarian critics.

A third, vital pair of dialectical terms is *mechanical* and *organic*. Coleridge used these in the discussion of forms – whether social forms, in the sense of social and political institutions; or artistic forms, as in the structure of a play, a picture, or a poem. The terms are largely self-explanatory: a mechanical form being constructed from without, according to preconceived rules and law; an organic form 'growing' and 'unfolding' from within, according to its own principles of development and function. Coleridge discusses these terms in his *Shakespearean Criticism*; in chapter XIV of the *Biographia* ('philosophic definitions of a poem and poetry'); and in the essay 'Hints towards a Theory of Life'. The terms have proved particularly influential in modern art and literary criticism, where the constant attack on traditional forms has required some 'dynamic' theory to account for the internal coherence of new and experimental styles and structures.

There are many other dialectical terms to be found in Coleridge: culture and civilisation, progress and permanency, heart and intellect, dream and reverie, allegory and symbol. But this pattern of thinking and enquiry is not limited to his prose. Many of his best poems also reveal a strong dialectical movement, either in their argument or their imagery: and frequently in both. The most obvious example, perhaps, is 'Dejection', where the oscillation between joy and sterile grief – seen as two possible responses to nature – commands the entire poem, and summons up an accompanying body of natural imagery, the painful calm of sunset and the releasing passion of storm. 'Frost at Midnight' contains a similar, but gentler movement, between an almost metaphysical concept of quiet and disquiet; and the conversation poems as a whole explore contrasting notions of being 'at home' in the human world, and 'homeless' or alienated within nature. Very comparable, but much more dramatic, poetic terms are at work in the *Mariner*, where imagery associated with the sun has a cruel and menacing aspect, and that of the Moon (and stars) is magical and healing. In the same way *Christabel* has a constant interplay between notions of guilt and innocence, and an accompanying body of sexual and animal emblems.

Such dialectical movements do not offer a final explanation or interpretation of Coleridge's poetry: but they suggest how it gains much of its power and coherence. They also show that it is the same, reconciling Coleridgean mind at work in the verse as in prose. Indeed, when he asks his readers in chapter XIV of the *Biographia* to enter upon the reading of his poems, with 'that willing suspension of disbelief for the moment, which constitutes poetic faith' (B 169), we find the poet and the critic are one.

III

For Coleridge the relationship between mind and nature is, at its deepest, a mystical one which could only be expressed in imaginative or symbolic terms. There is a transcendent or divine element within nature which finds a living response within the heart of every man, whatever his formal belief or unbelief. Mind and nature answer each other, and in that continuous living interchange, usually below the threshold of consciousness, is born what Coleridge called 'joy'. In the poet or artist, and pre-eminently in men like Shakespeare and Wordsworth, that interchange is made conscious and creative. But all men share in it. To lose such a consciousness, after having once experienced it – as Coleridge describes in 'Dejection' – was a crisis of spiritual significance in which the very 'ground of being' was challenged. Even human love fell back, feeble and helpless, before such a loss, as he wrote to Asra in April 1802:

> My genial Spirits fail –
> And what can these avail
> To lift the smoth'ring Weight from off my Breast?
> It were a vain Endeavour,
> Tho' I should gaze for ever
> On that Green Light which lingers in the West!
> I may not hope from outward Forms to win
> The Passion & the Life whose Fountains are within!
> These lifeless Shapes, around, below, Above,
> O what can they impart?
> When even the gentle Thought, that thou, my Love!
> Art gazing now, like me,
> And see'st the Heaven, I see –
> Sweet Thought it is – yet feebly stirs my Heart!
>
> (L II 791)

The 'fountain' imagery of this verse connects directly with the previous passages, describing the mystical quality of truth; and the experience of being lost and outcast, buried and isolated under one's own grief, is central to the mystical theme of the *Mariner*. Indeed the loss, or confirmation, of the mystical relationship with nature runs through Coleridge's poetry as a whole, even in the late works such as 'To Nature' and 'Limbo'.

But mysticism is not merely a poetical theme: it is fundamental to Coleridge's whole personality as a writer, and the

element of quest or pilgrimage which shapes his thought.
Throughout the notebooks there are passages where he medi-
tates on the workings of this mystical consciousness, and questions both its validity and its source. Whereas in the poetry it
tends to be associated with moments of acute personal crisis, in
the prose it is handled with greater calm and objectivity – and
for that very reason seems to reach out directly to the modern
reader. In his lonely rooms in Malta, in April 1805, he wrote:

> In looking at objects of Nature while I am thinking, as at
> yonder moon dim-glimmering thro' the dewy window-pane, I
> seem rather to be seeking, as it were *asking*, a symbolical lan-
> guage for something within me that already and forever ex-
> ists, than observing any thing new. Even when that latter is
> the case, yet still I have always an obscure feeling as if that
> new phenomenon were the dim Awaking of a forgotten or
> hidden Truth of my inner nature. (N II No. 2546)

It is difficult to categorise the mode of such an entry: is it
psychological enquiry? aesthetic investigation of the nature of
language? religious meditation? poetry or prayer? All these,
perhaps. The moonlit imagery certainly connects it with 'Frost
at Midnight', the *Mariner*, 'Dejection', and 'Limbo'. Yet it is
the very tentativeness, and scrupulousness of the terms – 'something that forever exists', 'an obscure feeling', 'dim Awaking'
– the lack of insistence and clamour, which carries such conviction to an agnostic and sceptical age.

By the time he came to write the *Biographia*, Coleridge had
undoubtedly located the source of his mysticism in his Protes-
tant inheritance (and thus in his father). Even more important,
he realised that it was this that led him towards European
thinkers, and the Transcendental tradition in Germany. In
chapter IX, he described how his own materialism and pantheism was held in check in the 1790s by inspirational writers such
as George Fox, the Quaker, and Jacob Boehme (1575–1624).
'For the writings of these mystics,' said Coleridge,

> acted in no slight degree to prevent my mind from being im-
> prisoned within the outline of a single dogmatic system. They
> contributed to keep alive the heart in the head; gave me an

indistinct, yet stirring and working presentment, that all the products of the mere reflective faculty partook of death, and were as the rattling twigs and sprays in winter into which a sap was yet to be propelled from some root to which I had not penetrated, if they were to afford my soul either food or shelter. (B 83)

That root was provided in 1799 by Immanuel Kant, whose writings took possession of Coleridge 'as with a giant's hand'; and later by Schelling, whose philosophy of the Unconscious gave system and rigour to Coleridge's intuitions.

As with Schlegel in the *Shakespearean Criticism*, so with Schelling in the philosophical sections of the *Biographia* (notably chapter XII), Coleridge has been accused of plagiarising from the German's writing. Certainly in a literary sense he borrowed, translated and adapted freely, and such passages have long been annotated in the standard modern editions of his work. But Coleridge never set himself up as a professional philosopher. He saw his debt to Germany in a much wider context: as part of his long personal journey towards a wholly new conception of man in nature, and as part of his life-long task to introduce such revolutionary ideas into the mainstream of English thought. Of Schelling's *Natur-Philosophie* (1797) and *System of Transcendental Idealism* (1800), he wrote with candour and considerable generosity:

. . . to Schelling we owe the completion, and the most important victories, of this revolution in philosophy. To me it will be happiness and honour enough should I succeed in rendering the system itself intelligible to my countrymen. . . . For readers in general, let whatever shall be found in this or any future work of mine that resembles or coincides with the doctrines of my German predecessor, though contemporary, be wholly attributed to him. . . . I regard truth as a divine ventriloquist: I care not from whose mouth the sounds are supposed to proceed, if only the words are audible and intelligible. (B 88–9)

Coleridge has in turn been seen as a pioneer of the European Existentialist movement, which is usually traced from Søren

Kierkegaard (1813–55), via Martin Heidegger (1899–1976), to Sartre, Camus, and modern theologians like Dietrich Bonhoeffer and Paul Tillich. Certainly the personal mysticism of Coleridge has several elements which are recognisably 'existential': the emphasis on the poet as the metaphysician of pure 'Being'; the dread in the face of non-Being; the anxiety or '*Angst*' when confronted by an apparently alien nature; the impulse to confirm or 'bless' what is central to the healing movement both in the *Mariner* and 'Dejection'.

Much of this is summed up in a remarkable passage at the end of the 'Treatise on Method', in which Coleridge seems to come forward and shake the reader with a series of direct, challenging questions:

> Hast thou ever raised thy mind to the consideration of EXISTENCE, in and by itself, as the mere act of existing? Hast thou ever said to thyself thoughtfully, IT IS! heedless in that moment, whether it were a man before thee, or a flower, or a grain of sand? . . . If thou hast indeed attained to this, thou wilt have felt the presence of a mystery. . . . The very words, There is nothing! or, There was a time, when there was nothing! are self-contradictory. There is that within us which repels the proposition with as full and instantaneous light, as if it bore evidence against the fact in the right of its own eternity.
>
> Not TO BE, then, is impossible: TO BE, incomprehensible. If thou hast mastered this intuition of absolute existence, thou wilt have learnt likewise, that it was this, and no other, which in the earlier ages seized the nobler minds, the elect among men, with a sort of sacred horror. This it was which first caused them to feel within themselves a something ineffably greater than their own individual nature. (F I 514)

Whether we compare that 'sacred horror' to the 'Dread' of Kierkegaard; the '*Angst*' of Heidegger ('*das Wovor der Angst ist das geworfene In-der-Welt-sein*' – 'the pain of *Angst*' arises from the sense of naked existence cast into 'psychic homelessness in the world'), or the '*Néant*' and '*nausée*' of Sartre, is perhaps immaterial. But it is an authentic expression of Coleridge's own struggle and sufferings; his search for the source of mystical experience; and his affirmation that the longing for the eternal and the infinite is the defining characteristic of man in nature.

One of the great, permanent generosities of Coleridge's work and thought is his acceptance that if he could not achieve this state of 'blessed' certainty and joy for himself he would strive to achieve it for those who came after him. This is what he promised his baby Hartley in 'Frost at Midnight'; but in a sense it is what he would want to promise – and give – to everyone who came in contact with his mind and spirit. It is this, more than anything, that gives his mysticism its curious quality of human *warmth*, that touches us more closely than many of the chillier contemporary exponents of Being and Non-Being.

> Therefore all seasons shall be sweet to thee,
> Whether the summer clothe the general earth
> With greenness, or the redbreast sit and sing
> Betwixt the tufts of snow on the bare branch
> Of mossy apple-tree, while the nigh thatch
> Smokes in the sun-thaw; whether the eave-drops fall
> Heard only in the trances of the blast,
> Or if the secret ministry of frost
> Shall hang them up in silent icicles,
> Quietly shining to the quiet Moon.

(P 242)

Elements of Coleridgean teaching

If Coleridge's writing does not form a unified system of thought in the philosophical sense, it does nevertheless compose a coherent body of ideas, an attitude to life and literature, which constitutes a doctrine or 'teaching'. Writing a decade after Coleridge's death, J. S. Mill described this teaching as 'the Germano-Coleridgean doctrine' which 'expresses the revolt of the human mind against the philosophy of the eighteenth century'. This doctrine, said Mill, 'is ontological, because that was experimental; conservative, because that was innovative; religious, because so much of that was infidel; . . . poetical, because that was matter-of-fact and prosaic.' We may add, too, that it is European, because that was insular; suffering and dark, because that was naïve and optimistic; human and personal, because that was abstract and mechanical. We should be aware of similar kinds of division in modern thought.

The central themes of Coleridge's teaching can be traced out by means of a number of keywords, which he spent much time exploring, redefining and illustrating so as to give them that imaginative life which is so important to his purpose as a writer. All but a few, such as 'clerisy' and 'Jacobin', have retained an active and vital presence in our language, and in re-examining them in the light of Coleridge's work, we are in fact re-examining the foundations of our own most precious beliefs and prejudices. His teaching, both in poetry and prose, does not necessarily ask for assent: but it asks for self-enquiry, a journey into ourselves, into the sources from which we draw value and meaning.

I

From his earliest plans to become a schoolmaster in the West Country to his latest series of lectures in 1817–19 on philosophy, general literature and Shakespeare, Coleridge was passionately committed to the idea of general *education*. He saw that revolutionary ideas of democracy, of Parliamentary reform, of social justice could have no real meaning without a radical re-examination of the function of education: what it really was, who needed it, and who was ultimately responsible for providing it. He consistently attacked the received eighteenth-century notions of education as a kind of social varnishing or finishing process (enshrined in the closed circuit of classical tutoring, Oxbridge and the Grand Tour) – 'perilously over-civilised, and most pitiably uncultivated!' Instead he pointed towards a much more fundamental process of cultivating and leading out (*e-duco*) qualities inherent in all young minds. The distinction he drew between those who were merely 'civilised' and those who were truly 'cultivated' had never been made so sharply in England before Coleridge, and it indicates a painful but growing awareness that the class basis of education must yield to a much more universal 'method' of imaginative training and self-development. The nature of that method, as applied to education, is one of the leading themes of volume III of *The Friend*, and it has borne fruit in a long line of writers on education, from Matthew Arnold to F. R. Leavis and Raymond Williams.

But it is crucial to realise that Coleridge did not come to this position through his political ideology (which grew paternalistic as he aged), but through his growing understanding, as a poet and philosophical critic, of the imaginative structure of the human mind. All men, all children, shared in the processes of nature. All minds were a natural growth, which was open to *cultivation*. Culture had for Coleridge almost a literally agricultural meaning: a process of sowing, nurturing, and gradual successive harvesting. He frequently retold his ironic reply to the radical Thelwall, who did not believe in 'planting' a child's mind with anything except 'rational' concepts until the age of discretion and choice. The result, said Coleridge, was perfectly illustrated by the weed-covered garden at Nether Stowey: 'I thought it unfair in me to prejudice the soil towards roses and strawberries' (T 105).

By contrast, in Lecture XI of his 'General Course on Literature' of 1818, he defined his universal approach to the education of young children, regarding only their natural powers and without reference to the accident of their birth or social situation:

In the education of children, love is first to be instilled, and out of love obedience is to be educed. Then impulse and power should be given to the intellect, and the ends of a moral being be exhibited. . . . We should address ourselves to those faculties in a child's mind, which are first awakened by nature, and consequently first admit of cultivation, that is to say, the memory and the imagination. The comparing power, the judgement, is not at that age active, and ought not to be forcibly excited, as is too frequently and mistakenly done in the modern systems of education, which can only lead to selfish views, debtor and creditor principles of virtue, and an inflated sense of merit. . . . The imagination is the distinguishing characteristic of man as a progressive being; and I repeat that it ought to be carefully guided and strengthened as the indispensable means and instrument of continued amelioration and refinement. (W IV 317–18)

The echo of this lecture can be caught in many later writers, who grew aware that in the general process of industrialisation and social upheaval, one kind of rational education was threatening to subdue another, more subtle, more imaginative kind. So the argument can be found continuing in the opening chapter of Dickens's *Hard Times* (1854), for example; or in J. S. Mill's *Autobiography* (1873); or in D. H. Lawrence's essay on childhood wonder, 'Hymns in a Man's Life' (1928); or in John Fowles's *The Aristos* (1964).

But for Coleridge the training of the imagination alone was not enough to produce the truly educated mind: it must also achieve what he called *method*. In *The Friend* he examines this in two senses: first, as an actual quality and habitual reflex of the mind itself; and second as the organisational principle which the mind applies to any body of knowledge 'in the constructions of science and literature'. In the first sense, which is really our subject here, method 'becomes natural to the mind which has become accustomed to contemplate not *things* only, or for their own sake alone, but likewise and chiefly the *relations* of things, either their relations to each other, or to the observer, or to the state and apprehension of the hearers' (F I 451).

For Coleridge, knowledge of any kind was still a 'thing' until it was mobilised, brought into fruitful 'relations', either with other areas of knowledge or with the observer's or listener's own experience. Method was the trained reflex of forming those relations, of fitting parts into a whole, of 'progressive transition' from simpler to more complex ideas. The methodical mind was one accustomed to shape information, to place it in significant order and sequence, and to relate it rapidly and accurately to wider frames of reference. The instinctive tendency of method was therefore to generalise on all experience, producing 'theories', 'laws', and finally hierarchies of knowledge. (Essays VI to XI of the 'Method' section explore the implications of this beyond the educational field, and examine it as the organisational principle common to all science, art and philosophy. Coleridge attacks, for instance, the claim of eighteenth-century botany to be a true science, as it is based on simple 'classification' rather than 'methodic' principle – as would eventually be provided by Mendelian genetics.)

For living examples of the methodically educated and uneducated mind, Coleridge turns to Shakespeare. He contrasts Hamlet's brooding account to Horatio of how he outwitted Rosencrantz and Guildenstern on the voyage to England (*Hamlet* v. ii); with Mistress Quickly's comically garrulous account to Falstaff of how he promised to marry her 'at the round table, by a seacoal fire, on Wednesday in Whitsun week . . .' (1 *Henry IV* II. i). Coleridge concludes that if we consider both speeches purely on their form, 'we should find both *immethodical*; Hamlet from the excess, Mrs Quickly from the want, of reflection and generalisation; and that Method, therefore, must result from the due mean or balance between our passive impressions and the mind's own reaction on the same' (F I 453).

In his treatment of method, with all its subtle ramifications, Coleridge was drawing equally on Platonic and Kantian notions. By contrasting the two ideals of imagination and method as the fundamental polarities of a true education, he forces us to consider it as a dynamic process, independent of the actual content of any given curriculum. Education, in other words, is not essentially about the subjects taught. It is about the process of teaching, learning and cultivating the mind. It is about the growth, nurture and harvest of a certain kind of personal awareness.

In a letter of July 1826, written to his nephew Edward, Coleridge tried to summarise his views in the form of three 'practical rules' which dispensed with the technical keywords of his more formal enquiries:

I. Remember, that whatever *is*, *lives*. A thing absolutely lifeless is inconceivable, except as a thought, image, or fancy, in some other being.

II. In every living form, the conditions of its *existence* are to be sought for in that which is *below* it; the grounds of its *intelligibility* in that which is *above* it.

III. Accustom your mind to distinguish the relations of things from the things themselves. Think often of the latter, independent of the former, in order that you may never . . . mistake mere relations for true and enduring realities: and with regard to *these* seek the solution of each in some higher reality. (C 183)

It is clear from this that the ultimate object, for Coleridge, of all education must be a hierarchy of awareness, whose final term will be, in some sense at least, religious.

But who then was responsible for education? Coleridge's answer to this is surprising, and in many ways still challengingly original. Among his contemporaries, the conservative thinkers (appalled by the impact of French Revolutionary and 'atheistical' doctrines) saw education as the essential business of the Church. The six British universities (until the founding of London University in 1836) remained religious institutions, staffed by clergymen. Radical thinkers, on the other hand, saw a wholly secular future for education, in the direct control of the State.

Coleridge disagreed with both sides. He proposed that the business of education should be independent of both Church and State: that it should form a separate 'estate of the Realm' – the *clerisy*, or 'National Church'. This body should comprise scholars, scientists, learned priests and laymen, schoolmasters, writers, artists, teachers and thinkers of every kind, irrespective of their formal religious persuasions – 'the learned of all denominations'.

In *On the Constitution of Church and State*, Coleridge presented this national clerisy as the great reconciling and sustaining body within the Constitution as a whole, which would balance those forces of permanency and progression which are continuously in conflict within the nation; and at times of great change, most acutely so. The clerisy would be the dynamic centre of renewal within national life, its object 'to secure and improve that civilisation, without which the nation could be neither permanent nor progressive'. And that civilisation was, of course, to be 'grounded in *cultivation*, in the harmonious development of those qualities and faculties that characterise our *humanity*' (C 44, 42–3).

A clerisy, in the Coleridgean sense, has never been instituted in Britain; but the influence of the idea has been enormous – as traced for example by Raymond Williams in his essay 'Two Literary Critics', from *Culture and Society* (1958). The very breadth of the terms employed, the boldness of the conception, has made it endlessly re-applicable from one generation of critics and writers to the next, as a test of educational shortcomings.

In the first place, Coleridge insisted that the clerisy must be a comprehensive body, comprising

> ... the learned of all denominations; – the sages and professors of the law and jurisprudence; of medicine and physiology; of music; of military and civil architecture; of the physical sciences; with the mathematical as the common *organ* of the preceding; in short all the so called liberal arts and sciences, the possession and application of which constitute the civilisation of a country, as well as the Theological. (C 46–7)

There was to be no 'two cultures', as in C. P. Snow's famous polemic; but Coleridge's proposal clearly implies, equally, that any Leavisite notion of a purely literary culture is inadequate; and so too is a clerisy that, in our own time, does not include the new young arts and disciplines of the media – of radio and television; of newspaper and magazine journalism; of advertising; of records; of film-making. All this is part of the nation's central consciousness – the adapting, balancing, reconciling power. (But it also raises a disturbing and unfashionable question: is it possible for a clerisy to function like this as a purely secular force, without any kind of religious beliefs held in common?)

In the second place, Coleridge emphasised the responsibility of the clerisy to every level of society – not just to an 'élite', as we should now say. It must work like a yeast or sap through the remotest fibres of the national body, bringing justice, enlightenment and social cohesion. In this sense it was a 'permanent class, or order' with distinct duties, the 'final intention of the whole order' being

> to preserve the stores, to guard the treasures, of past civilisation, and thus to bind the present with the past; to perfect and add to the same, and thus to connect the present with the future; but especially to diffuse through the whole community, and to every native entitled to its laws and rights, that

quantity and quality of knowledge which was indispensable both for the understanding of those rights, and for the performance of the duties correspondent. (C 43–4)

Again, this makes a current debate, such as that between state and private education, seem curiously limited, almost a matter of form. What matters, says Coleridge, is the degree to which the clerisy are performing – or are able to perform – the full range of their duties throughout society. Where they are failing, it is the State's responsibility to intercede; where they are succeeding, it is the State's duty to respect their independence. But in the end the clerisy can only be answerable to itself: individual culture, with its continuous development and minute adaptations, cannot be imposed according to some collective, national or economic purpose. The clerisy must guard its independence, and sense of duty to itself, as jealously as a man would guard his own conscience. If the clerisy fail a nation, who is left to save it? *Quis custodiet custodes?*

One answer to this question is the political revolutionary – or *Jacobin*. No writer of Coleridge's generation – Southey, Wordsworth, Godwin, Mackintosh; or later Hazlitt, Cobbett, Shelley – could avoid the French Revolution, and the figure of the Jacobin revolutionary (Marat, Robespierre, Saint-Just), as a possible model for social change.

Coleridge returned again and again in his writings to the challenge posed by various forms of English Jacobinism. As a young man in the early 1790s, he undoubtedly had great hopes of the French Revolution, and he later recalled how he had 'aided the Jacobins, by witty sarcasms & subtle reasonings & declamations full of genuine feeling against all Rulers & against all established Forms' (L II 1001). Yet even in the angry *Lectures 1795* his Christian radicalism leads him to insist that revolution must begin in the heart and mind, before it can take any political form. He did not even accept the progressive intellectual revolution proposed by Godwin.

That general Illumination should precede Revolution, is a truth as obvious, as that the Vessel should be cleansed before we fill it with a pure Liquor. But the mode of diffusing it is not discoverable with equal facility. . . . The Author of an essay on political Justice considers private Societies as the sphere of real utility – that (each one illuminating those immediately beneath him) Truth by a gradual descent may at last reach the lowest order. But this is rather plausible than just or practicable. Society as at present constituted does not resemble a chain that ascends in a continuity of Links. . . . alas! between the Parlour and the Kitchen, the Tap and the Coffee-Room – there is a gulph that may not be passed. He would appear to me to have adopted the best as well as the most benevolent mode of diffusing Truth, who uniting the zeal of the Methodist with the views of the Philosopher, should be *personally* among the Poor, and teach them their *Duties* in order that he may render them susceptible of their Rights. (LPR 43)

This characteristic emphasis on duty led Coleridge to attack the 'rights of man' philosophy of Rousseau and Tom Paine in the pages of *The Friend*. Meanwhile the phases of his disillusion with France, as the mouthpiece of liberty, are eloquently traced in the short prose Preface to 'France: an Ode' (1798) – a description which summarises the experience of an entire generation. This sad but honest 'recantation' should be compared with the bitter attacks later made by younger writers like Shelley in the Preface to *The Revolt of Islam* (1817), and Hazlitt in *The Spirit of the Age* (1825).

Coleridge's criticism of a government built exclusively 'on personal and natural rights' is hard for us to understand in its negative aspect. We stand on the far side of a gulf of social change, which in the event was not achieved by violent Jacobin revolution, but by a process of continual agitation and adaptation, the extension of the franchise and the formation of new institutions like the trades unions, or the whole machinery of the Welfare State, much of which Coleridge foresaw and prophetically supported. But in *The Friend* Coleridge envisaged a degree of commitment to social justice on the part of government that is altogether remarkable at a time when most liberal thinkers were prepared to go little further than the idea (held rather nervously) of Parliamentary reform. 'With states, as well as individuals,' he wrote, 'not to be progressive is to be retrograde.' He proposed four *positive* ends of government:

> *1st.* to make the means of subsistence more easy to each indi-
> vidual. *2d.* that in addition to the necessaries of life he should
> derive from the union and division of labour a share of the
> comforts and conveniences which humanise and ennoble his
> nature; and at the same time the power of perfecting himself
> in his own branch of industry by having those things which
> he needs provided for him by others among his fellow
> citizens; including the tools and raw or manufactured mate-
> rials necessary to his own employment. *3dly.* The hope of
> bettering his own condition and that of his children. . . .
> Lastly, the development of those faculties which are essential
> to his human nature by the knowledge of his moral and reli-
> gious duties, and the increase of his intellectual powers in as
> great a degree as is compatible with the other ends of social
> union. . . . (F I 252–3)

This is a remarkable document, particularly in its whole attitude to the right to work. But of course it studiedly avoids the
'rights'-centred language of the Jacobin and revolutionary
democrat. Coleridge always emphasised the primacy of social
'duty' – something that sharply challenges modern Western
orthodoxy. (And the question remains open even now, whether
a free society can sustain itself purely on the concept of individual 'right'.)

This was, first, because Coleridge was part of a generation
that had been deeply marked and frightened by the spectacle of
revolutionary violence in France. Second, he held an 'organic'
view of society, in which the violent assertion of rights (however
idealistic in themselves) would have a profoundly damaging,
stultifying effect on the actual growth of 'positive institutions',
and the long-term improvement of social relations. But third,
and most important of all, Coleridge believed that Jacobinism
was based on a fundamental misconception about State power:
that external political machinery could transform the inward nature of man: 'that all, or the greater part of, the happiness or
misery, virtue or vice, of mankind, depends on forms of government' (E I 368). Jacobinism, in action, becomes the Juggernaut
of pure, abstract reason, crushing everything in its path.

Yet if Coleridge rejected the Jacobin model, he remained deeply tinged by his early vision of liberty: for all such as he, 'hopes will burn like the Greek fire, hard to be extinguished, and easily rekindling' (E I 368). Something of this still touches off the naked anger against the 'OVERBALANCE OF THE COMMER-CIAL SPIRIT' in his pamphlets against child labour; and in the second *Lay Sermon* where he attacks the spirit of callous exploitation which regards poverty and social evil as 'so much superfluous steam ejected by the Escape Pipes and Safety Valves of a self-regulating Machine' (LS 205). In this we can trace the language of social protest that will emerge in Carlyle's attack on the 'cash-nexus'; and the revulsion of men like Ruskin and William Morris from a brutal, mechanised, competitive industrial society. Remarking how often politicians of all persuasions refer to 'things always finding their level', Coleridge wrote bitterly and passionately:

> But Persons are not *Things* – but Man does not find his level. Neither in body nor in soul does the Man find his level! After a hard and calamitous season, during which the thousand Wheels of some vast manufactory had remained silent as a frozen water-fall, be it that plenty has returned and that Trade has once more become brisk and stirring: go, ask the overseer, and question the parish doctor, whether the workman's health and temperance with the staid and respectful Manners best taught by the inward dignity of conscious self-support, have found *their* level again! Alas! I have more than once seen a group of children in Dorsetshire, during the heat of the dog-days, each with its little shoulders up to its ears, and its chest pinched inward, the very habit and *fixtures*, as it were, that had been impressed on their frames by the former ill-fed, ill-clothed, and unfuelled winters. But as with the Body, so or still worse with the Mind. (LS 206–7)

How close, after all, is this to that most Jacobinical of poets, Shelley, who wrote in *The Mask of Anarchy* only two years later (1819), in answer to the question, 'What art thou Freedom?' – 'Thou art clothes, and fire, and food / For the trampled multitude – / No – in countries that are free / Such starvation cannot be /As in England now we see.' The main difference perhaps is that Shelley had fled to Italy; Coleridge had remained to teach, 'pitching his tent', in Hazlitt's final consolatory phrase, 'upon the barren waste without, and having no abiding place or city of refuge!'

II

But Coleridge considered a completely different kind of answer to the question, *Quis custodiet custodes?* When dealing with the ultimate problems of truth, value, meaning, and moral justice for man in society, all the Romantics eventually found themselves turning towards quite another figure: neither the teacher, the philosopher, nor the revolutionary politician – but the creative artist, the *poet*. Shelley's provocative formulation (itself taken from William Godwin) that 'Poets are the unacknowledged legislators of the World' is the most celebrated of these claims.

In chapter XIV of the *Biographia*, Coleridge put forward the poet (using the word in its largest sense, to include equally Plato, Wordsworth and the author of the Book of Isaiah) as another more permanent reconciling and unifying influence in society; one who brings man, as it were, to his highest pitch:

> The poet, described in ideal perfection, brings the whole soul of man into activity, with the subordination of its faculties to each other, according to their relative worth and dignity. He diffuses a tone and spirit of unity that blends and (as it were) fuses, each into each, by that synthetic and magical power to which we have exclusively appropriated the name of imagination. This power . . . reveals itself in the balance and reconciliation of opposite or discordant qualities: of sameness, with difference; of the general, with the concrete; the idea, with the image; the individual, with the representative; the sense of novelty and freshness, with old and familiar objects; a more than usual state of emotion, with more than usual order; judgement ever awake and steady self-possession, with enthusiasm and feeling profound or vehement. . . .
> (B 173–4)

A detailed commentary on this passage has been given by

I. A. Richards in his *Coleridge on Imagination* (1934). What concerns us here is the description of an overall process: an intensification of the state of being, which we can call psychological, or spiritual: a heightened activity and an expansion of the conditions of reality: a greater and more complex sense of truth. 'Ideally' the poet gives us all that: and the clear implication is that he turns us from limited social beings into visionary spiritual ones.

Much of Coleridge's literary criticism is really directed towards discovering the source of this power and authority in the poet, rather than analysing the qualities of individual poets. His grand exemplars are Shakespeare and Wordsworth; and to a lesser degree Milton. But he also draws continuously on his own experience as a creative writer, in a way that connects with later deeply autobiographical critics of life and literature (it is almost impossible to make the distinction here) as for example, D. H. Lawrence writing about Hardy or Poe, and Jean-Paul Sartre writing about Flaubert or Baudelaire. In each case we feel that the whole man, the whole personality, is engaged: indeed more than engaged, is gambled, thrown down as an absolute stake without reserves.

For all its humour, and parenthetical pottering, and little deprecatory gestures of literary chit-chat, this is everywhere true of Coleridge's *Biographia*. Great chapters, like XV and XVII on the sources of power in the poet's language, or chapter XVIII on the psychological origins of the poet's form and metre as 'an interpenetration of passion and will', are written with a philosophical conviction and degree of personal testimony – of bearing witness to primary truths painfully unearthed – that is quite new in English criticism; and rare to this day.

But we can find this intense commitment to the poet's function emerging much earlier: most strikingly in the letters written to William Sotheby in 1802, from Keswick, at the very height of the crisis which produced 'Dejection'. We have already seen what Coleridge wrote of the poet as metaphysician. But he also criticised the artificiality and *lack of risk* in a poet like William Bowles, and by implication the entire eighteenth-century tradition of the poet as genteel onlooker, commentator and 'civilised' spectator:

There reigns thro' all the blank verse poems [of Bowles] such a perpetual trick of *moralising* every thing – which is very well, occasionally – but never to see or describe any interesting appearance in nature, without connecting it by dim analogies with the moral world, proves faintness of Impression. Nature has her proper interest; & he will know what it is, who believes & feels, that every Thing has a Life of its own, & that we are all *one Life*. A Poet's *Heart & Intellect* should be *combined, intimately* combined & *unified*, with the great appearances in Nature – & not merely held in solution & loose mixture with them, in the shape of formal Similies. . . . The truth is – Bowles has indeed the *sensibility* of a poet; but he has not the *Passion* of a great Poet. His latter Writings all want *native* Passion – Milton here & there supplies him with an appearance of it – but he has no native Passion, because he is not a Thinker – & has probably weakened his Intellect by the haunting Fear of becoming extravagant. (L II 864)

How revealing that last remark is: it points to a whole Romantic tradition of 'fine excess' (Keats) which reaches its climax in Rimbaud's proposition that the poet should make himself a 'seer' through a prolonged and deliberate disordering of the senses – a proposition that the Coleridge of 'Kubla Khan' would have understood instinctively, if not agreed with. Yet the whole passage is central to Coleridge's faith in the poet: that he *combines* thought and 'passion, heart and intellect, man and nature.

The concept of the 'one Life' is close to the very heart of this faith. At one level of meaning, it is almost purely technical and linguistic: the Romantic poet does not distance himself from his subject by 'formal Similies', analogies, moralising comparisons: he enters into the very life of the subject, by re-enactment, by metaphor, by symbolic correspondence. As Coleridge wrote of Shakespeare's *Venus and Adonis*: 'You seem to be *told* nothing, but to see and hear everything' (B 177).

At a second level, it is clearly a social statement, an affirmation of shared experience and need. It is the equivalent to Wordsworth's poet 'speaking in the language of men'. But in chapter XVII of the *Biographia*, Coleridge goes to great lengths to distinguish this notion of vital community from a narrow 'rustic' interpretation of the 'one Life', as the exclusive property of a rural or peasant society, and a language and sensibility generated purely by contact with the 'beautiful and permanent forms of nature'. This may be called the Lake Poets' heresy: and Coleridge did not share it.

Instead, he insisted that such a community of language and feeling belongs ultimately to the 'educated mind', which is not dependent on class or occupation but on personal cultivation. This Romantic dispute about the social location, as it were, of the 'one Life' continues: and every attempt by writers and artists to go back to their country roots – from William Morris to the Brotherhood of Ruralists – re-enacts it. The ultimate source of the dispute is Rousseau. But the professional implications for the poet (and the artist generally) are nowhere so clearly demonstrated as in the ideological clash between Coleridge and Wordsworth.

At a third level, the 'one Life' is a mystical statement of belief that recalls William Blake's great cry of affirmation in *The Marriage of Heaven and Hell*: 'For every thing that lives is Holy!' It is interesting to find Coleridge re-stating this as a critic, at the very time, in 'Dejection', that he was questioning it as a poet. Yet it would be simplistic to suppose that such beliefs do not have to be struggled for ceaselessly. In fact his most moving and explicit commitment to the 'one Life' comes in a suggestive addition to the poem of 1795, 'The Eolian Harp', which Coleridge did not make until 1828, six years before his death. It reads:

> O! the one Life within us and abroad,
> Which meets all motions and becomes its soul,
> A light in sound, a sound-like power in light,
> Rhythm in all thought, and joyance every where –
> Methinks, it should have been impossible
> Not to love all things in a world so fill'd;
> Where the breeze warbles, and the mute still air
> Is Music slumbering on her instrument.

(P 101)

The view of the poet's powers which Coleridge had already established in 1802, and which he was later to test and explore in detail with reference to Wordsworth in volume II of the *Biographia*, has four cardinal elements: First, that his medium – language, imagery and metre – is generated directly by the shaping power of his passion, not by traditional forms. Thus his poetry, at its highest, is a permanent and elemental expression of man's nature. Second, that the poet's 'heart and intellect' combine with the forms of the natural world, rather than moralising on them at a distance, and this interpenetration of subject and object gives living proof of the new relations between man and nature which European philosophers had already theoretically stated. Third, that the poet's highest faculty is the highest and most progressive faculty in man: the imagination. Fourth, that the more the poet becomes critically conscious of his powers (and responsibilities), the more he also becomes a metaphysician, whose duty to society – and this is really Coleridge's answer to Plato – is to show how 'every Thing has a Life of its own, & that we are all one Life'.

Such ideas naturally led Coleridge to place great value on the whole notion of *organic* form or unity. The term 'organic', as the loose description of a certain kind of society, closely knit, slow to change, based on agricultural rather than industrial processes and rhythms, had already been popularised by Edmund Burke. Coleridge, as we have seen, used it in this sense too in his political writings and *Lay Sermons*, though emphasising more the metaphorical meaning of fruitful and harmonious growth: i.e. a progressive rather than static society. But because of his philosophical training, Coleridge pursued the underlying dualism between organic and mechanical as a fundamental principle of Romantic literary form. This becomes really the basis of his entire *Shakespearean Criticism*.

The English and French eighteenth-century view of Shakespeare, with its tradition of textual emendation, and cutting scenes in order to conform to the classical unities of Greek or French drama (time, place, action), was based according to Coleridge on a wholly inadequate and mechanical concept of dramatic form. The accepted view was that Shakespeare was an unschooled, natural 'genius', who lacked the civilised 'judgement' to discipline and shape his plays: 'a sort of African nature, fertile in beautiful monsters . . .' (S I 198), whereas Coleridge dedicated all his lectures, from 1808 onwards, to proving 'that in all points from the most important to the most minute, the judgement of Shakespeare is commensurate with his genius':

> The true ground of the mistake, as has been well remarked by a continental critic, lies in the confounding mechanical regularity with organic form. The form is mechanic when on any given material we impress a pre-determined form, not necessarily arising out of the properties of the material, as when to a mass of wet clay we give whatever shape we wish it to retain when hardened. The organic form, on the other hand, is innate; it shapes as it develops itself from within, and the fullness of its development is one and the same with the perfection of its outward form. Such is the life, such the form. Nature, the prime genial artist, inexhaustible in diverse powers, is equally inexhaustible in forms. Each exterior is the physiognomy of the being within, its true image reflected and thrown out from the concave mirror. And even such is the appropriate excellence of her chosen poet, or our own Shakespeare, himself a nature humanised, a genial understanding directing self-consciously a power and an implicit wisdom deeper than consciousness. (S I 198)

This kind of 'organic' argument leads to a revolution in such things as the staging and editing of Shakespeare; the appreciation of scene shifts and the alteration of mood and pace; the connection between a character and the image-patterns of his speech; and the whole notion of spiritual development and internal coherence in great tragic figures like Macbeth, Hamlet and Lear. All this is part of Coleridge's legacy to Shakespearean critics or directors like A. C. Bradley, Harley Granville-Barker, G. Wilson Knight, Wolfgang Clemen, Jan Kott and Peter Brook.

Yet the source of the argument is plainly philosophical: it arises out of Coleridge's interest in the currents of European post-Kantian theory, and in fact – as the tell-tale phrase, 'as has been well remarked by a continental critic' (which of course is part of a lecture note, not a published essay) suggests – the first part of the quotation is translated, and adapted, from

Schlegel's lectures (including the wet clay image); while the second is based on Schelling's theories of the Unconscious in Art, from Part IV of his *Transcendental Idealism*.

This close grounding in European theory is precisely what Coleridge has led us to expect. He tells us time and time again that only new philosophic concepts like 'organic form' can break down the traditional English boundaries between disciplines, and help us grasp the essential coherence of his discussions of education, or Jacobinism, or poetry. Yet in every case, not only does he make them completely and distinctively his own: but through his native gifts as a writer he conveys them with unforgettable freshness and vigour – 'on the pulses' of his own experience, in the Keatsian phrase.

In the *Shakespearean Criticism* this is most evident in the individual lecture notes on *Hamlet, Lear, Macbeth, Romeo and Juliet* and *The Tempest*. But we can take a single remark on two lines of *Venus and Adonis* (from the 1808 lectures) as an example of Coleridge working at 'the most minute' level to establish the organic, unifying texture of Shakespeare's poetry. Adonis has just left the 'enamoured goddess' in the thickening dusk of evening: 'Look! how a bright star shooteth from the sky, / So glides he in the night from Venus' eye.' Coleridge's magical and deeply empathetic comment (a poet on a poet, without question) runs: 'How many images and feelings are here brought together without effort and without discord – the beauty of Adonis – the rapidity of his flight – the yearning yet hopelessness of the enamoured gazer – and a shadowy ideal character thrown over the whole' (S I 189).

The unity which Coleridge demonstrates here is especially between concrete image and a series of abstract qualities – beauty, rapidity, yearning, the shadowy ideal; but it is also, at a more subtle level, between Shakespeare's 'aloof' artistry as a poet, and his absolute identification with the feelings of his 'dramatic' heroine, Venus. The images actually appear to be generated, through Venus's own eyes, like so many tears. It is in fact a model of Shakespeare's method of creating dramatic character throughout the plays: one distinct type of organic form. (Did Keats somehow hear this comment before he wrote his last sonnet, 'Bright Star'?)

III

The kind of philosophic criticism which Coleridge was able to bring to the poetry of Shakespeare and Wordsworth gave rise to a wholly new notion, for the English Romantics, of what language itself was doing when put to work at maximum power and resource. Coleridge came to describe this heightened condition of language as the creation of *symbols*.

One of the last concepts to evolve in his writing, it is the result of another characteristic shift in his frame of reference between 1814 and 1818, from the literary-philosophical to the openly religious. We have already cited his meditation, from the notebooks of 1805, on the sensation of seeking or asking for 'a symbolical language' while in the act of contemplating the 'dim-glimmering moon', in Malta. But it is not until ten years later, in chapter IX of the *Biographia*, that he explicitly examines the symbol as a heightened form of meaning; and even here its value as a purveyor of truth is enigmatic.

> An IDEA, in the highest sense of that word, cannot be conveyed but by a symbol; and, except in geometry, all symbols of necessity involve an apparent contradiction. . . . Veracity does not consist in saying, but in the intention of communicating truth; and the philosopher who cannot utter the whole truth without conveying falsehood and at the same time, perhaps, exciting the most malignant passions, is constrained to express himself mythically or equivocally. (B 85)

The implication would seem to be here that the symbol holds back, hides, or conveniently suspends meaning, rather like a secret code or Masonic gesture. It is a containing device rather than a productive one: in Blakean terms it is a cistern rather than a fountain.

But by 1816 the symbol has become one of the great positive ideas which Coleridge advances in the *Statesman's Manual*. It is the answer to the narrow, mechanical approach to religious truth which he sees as throttling society in utilitarianism; but much more, it is the claim that language can be charged with levels of meaning which are not rationally 'closed' or limited in interpretation.

A hunger-bitten and idea-less philosophy naturally produces a starveling and comfortless religion. It is among the miseries of the present age that it recognises no medium between *Literal* and *Metaphorical*. Faith is either to be buried in the dead letter, or its name and honours usurped by a counterfeit product of the mechanical understanding, which in the blindness of self-complacency confounds SYMBOLS with ALLEGORIES. Now an Allegory is but a translation of abstract notions into a picture-language which is itself nothing but an abstraction from objects of the senses; the principal being more worthless even than its phantom proxy.... On the other hand a Symbol ... is characterised by a translucence of the Special in the Individual or of the General in the Especial or of the Universal in the General. Above all by the translucence of the Eternal through and in the Temporal. It always partakes of the Reality which it renders intelligible; and while it enunciates the whole, abides itself as a living part in that Unity, of which it is the representative. (LS 30)

The central idea here is that of translucence, of something greater shining through something lesser. The symbol is an active radiation, or outflowing, of meaning from a higher (unseen) source through a lower (visible) one. (The modern physicist's contrast between inert and radioactive materials would have been perfect for Coleridge's distinction.) As so often in Coleridge the roots of the idea go back to his earliest poetry, and we can glimpse it in his contemplation of the river Otter; his lingering fascination in 'This Lime-Tree Bower' with the 'deep radiance' of the sun on the 'ancient ivy'; or his mysterious reverence for the green and silent dell in the Quantocks ('Fears in Solitude') which, 'Bathed by the mist, is fresh and delicate / As vernal corn-field, or the unripe flax, / When, through its half-transparent stalks, at eve, / The level sunshine glimmers with green light' (P 257).

But now, by contrasting it with allegory, the translucent power of the symbol is given a precise formulation, both at a philosophical and a linguistic level. Since the word 'symbol' has entered so constantly – and loosely – into contemporary speech, first through a literary awareness of the French nineteenth-century Symbolist poets, and second through a popularisation of psychoanalytic, or Freudian, symbolism (especially dream symbols) dating from the early 1920s, it is worth considering very closely what Coleridge originally meant.

In an allegory, as he says, an abstract idea is simply 'translated' into picture language. The sun 'stands for' God; or the moon 'stands for' the imagination. The relation between the two is direct and 'mechanical', there is no interpenetration of identity, no imaginative increase of scale, no linguistic 'charge'. It is what we would call a closed, 'one-to-one' relationship. It is what Coleridge later calls 'an empty echo'. (It is ironic to reflect that probably the most famous twentieth-century symbol of all – the 'phallic symbol' – is almost universally interpreted allegorically in Coleridge's sense. The phallic symbol is thought literally 'to stand for' the male organ, the erect penis. This is a delightful popular misconception roughly equivalent to thinking that Frankenstein is the Monster.)

But the true symbol is not a straight 'translation'. There is no one-to-one relation of meaning, that can be directly decoded. The symbol is a living part of that which it symbolises: there is, to some degree, an interpenetration of identities, a continuity of meaning. We are here very close to the later French poetic system of universal *correspondances* which was first set forth, probably by Gérard de Nerval, in *Les Chimérès* (1854), but given currency by Baudelaire's 1857 poem '*Correspondances*', which begins

> La Nature est un temple où de vivants piliers
> Laissent parfois sortir de confuses paroles;
> L'homme y passe à travers des forêts de symboles
> Qui l'observent avec des regards familiers. . . .

> (Nature is a temple wherein the living pillars sometimes let out a confusion of words; man moves through them passing forests of symbols which gaze down on him with a look of recognition. . . .)

One wonders how literary history might have changed if Baudelaire had chosen to translate Coleridge rather than De Quincey.

This continuity of meaning in the symbol, with the greater always being expressed through the lesser, is what gives it its special power. Coleridge himself uses a metaphor – of light, and translucence – to express the radiant, charged quality of symbolic language. The original metaphor of the fountain 'which overflows' is equally apt. But the crucial idea is that the symbol is *inexhaustible* of meaning. Because it derives its power to signify from a higher dimension of truth, 'the General in the Especial, or the Universal in the General' – or the infinite in the finite – it cannot be emptied of meaning at the level at which it is presented, visibly as it were, to the reader. We cannot finally say, 'it stands for *that*' – only that 'it draws its power from *there*'.

Once again Blake throws light on the mystical assumptions underlying this position, when he writes in *The Marriage of Heaven and Hell*: 'If the doors of perception were cleansed every thing would appear to man as it is, infinite. For man has closed himself up, till he sees all things thro' narrow chinks of his cavern.' The cavern reminds us of Kubla's 'caves of ice'; and ultimately of the philosopher's cave with its shadows of reality, in Plato. The chinks recall all the transcendent 'glimmerings' in Coleridge's poetry.

Coleridge never went on to elaborate a complete system of symbolism, though he observed in the *Statesman's Manual* that 'True natural philosophy is comprised in the study of science and the language of *symbols*'. Yet it is impossible to imagine the development of the religious thought of Carlyle, J. H. Newman or Dean Inge without Coleridgean symbolism, and the very survival of Biblical texts in the onslaught of nineteenth-century scientific materialism ('no medium between *Literal* and *Metaphorical*') would have been doubtful without the conception of symbolic language. Even more, probably the most powerful and fruitful movement in modern literary criticism – certainly as rich in insights as Marxism or Structuralism – has arisen from a popular combination of Coleridgean, Jungian and Freudian symbolism, at first in technical works such as Maud Bodkin's *Archetypal Patterns in Poetry* (1927), but largely as a general awareness among English and American critics of the symbolic potential within all literature, both poetry and prose. Not the least writer to benefit from this has, of course, been Coleridge himself: for what are his suns and moons, his rivers and dells, his storms and starlight, his Albatross and Abyssinian maid -- if not

> the living *educts* of the Imagination; of that reconciling and mediatory power, which incorporating the Reason in Images of the Sense, and organising (as it were) the flux of the Senses by the permanence and self-circling energies of the Reason, gives birth to a system of symbols, harmonious in themselves, and consubstantial with the truths, of which they are the *conductors*. (LS 29)

Coleridge's theory of symbolic language was explicitly developed in the religious context of the *Statesman's Manual*, and it is clearly based on a mystical or transcendental attitude to nature. But it also reflects a mystical attitude to the powers of the human mind. 'For,' as he wrote, 'all things that surround us, and all things that happen unto us, have . . . all one common final cause: namely, the increase of Consciousness, in such wise, that whatever part of the terra incognita of our nature the increased consciousness discovers, our will may conquer and bring into subjection to itself under the sovreignty of reason' (LS 89). No part of that *terra incognita*, that unknown land, so consistently fascinated Coleridge as the realm of *dreams*, and all the related territories of reverie, day-dream, opium dream, hallucination and supposedly visionary experience.

His notebooks, especially between 1802 and 1806, contain such detailed documentation of these materials that it is surprising he never wrote a formal treatise, like Baudelaire's *Les Paradis artificiels*, or a 'confession' of his opium experiences, like De Quincey, or even that 'critical essay on the uses of the supernatural in poetry and the principles that regulate its introduction' which he had promised in a tantalising aside in chapter XIII of the *Biographia*. Nevertheless no other English Romantic writer makes such dramatic use of dreams in his work, and it is evident that Coleridge had recognised their symbolic function long before he had elaborated his distinction between symbol and allegory, so that many of his best poems have a structural dependence on dream or visionary sequences.

The *Mariner*, which was originally subtitled 'A Poet's

Reverie', uses the early dream of the ship's crew, together with the Mariner's later vision of the two Spirits in Part VI (after he has collapsed in a swoon) to deepen our understanding of the descending levels of the action, so that we seem to move continually inward and downward, from one threshold of consciousness to the next. (One recalls Keats's mention of 'first and second consciousness' as one of Coleridge's conversational subjects.) In a different way, dreams are crucial to *Christabel*, and the theme of spiritual seduction.

In the most famous of all Coleridge's dream poems, indeed the most famous dream in English literature, 'Kubla Khan', the dream is not a structural device, but the actual precondition of creativity. It is the poet himself who claims to have been dreaming, and in the Preface in the 1816 edition Coleridge presented the piece 'rather as a psychological curiosity, than on the ground of any supposed *poetic* merits' (P 295). We are here dealing with a phenomenon apparently prefiguring the *écriture automatique* of the French Surrealists. Coleridge's unconscious seems to have combined two main streams of imagery: from his reading of the Xanadu description in Purchas, and from his daily walking among the wooded hills and deep water-threaded dells of the Quantocks. After taking opium in the lonely farmhouse, explained Coleridge,

> The Author continued for about three hours in a profound sleep, at least of the external senses, during which time he has the most vivid confidence, that he could not have composed less than from two to three hundred lines; if that indeed can be called composition in which all the images rose up before him as *things*, with a parallel production of the correspondent expressions, without any sensation or consciousness of effort. On awaking he appeared to himself to have a distinct recollection of the whole, and taking his pen, ink, and paper, instantly and eagerly wrote down the lines that are here preserved. At this moment he was unfortunately called out by a person on business from Porlock. . . . (P 296)

So, we are to believe, the rest of the poem was lost. Coleridge's account is almost as interesting as the poem, though it is difficult to accept that the chanting, hypnotic, highly finished language of 'Kubla Khan' is *literally* as Coleridge dreamt it.

What does appear distinctly dream-like, however, is the sequence of the verse. One subject drifts into another – the sacred river, the romantic chasm, the voices prophesying war, the caves of ice, the Abyssinian maid, the milk of Paradise – without demonstrable logic or progression. It is possible to provide this logic by arguing that all the images have a primarily sexual meaning; or that the poem recounts a hallucinatory walk through a formal garden (like nearby Stourhead) under the influence of drugs, and that it really belongs to the genre of eighteenth-century topographical poems; or that the poem is a highly philosophical allegory of the imagination in the process of creating a work of art (the 'sunny pleasure dome'). All of these explanations are satisfactory up to a point (nor are they mutually exclusive); yet the poem is oddly resistant to them – or rather it swallows them up, and finally returns to its original enigmatic condition. In fact the poem is labyrinthine, endless, *fanciful*, exactly as in a dream: studying it leaves one with a curious sense of unease and claustrophobia. One's final impression is that 'Kubla Khan' is a psychological 'rare device', like the *carceri*, or imaginary prisons, of the Italian topographical artist, Giambattista Piranesi, rather than a genuinely symbolic poem.

Coleridge seems to have underlined his own doubts about the vision by placing after it, in the 1816 edition of his poems, the agonised and very deliberate verse of 'The Pains of Sleep', which he introduced as 'a fragment of a very different character, describing with equal fidelity the dream of pain and disease'. In other words, the ecstasies of 'Kubla Khan' may have been false – an 'artificial paradise' in the derogatory sense – while the agonies of opium-tortured sleep were undoubtedly real:

> But yester-night I prayed aloud
> In anguish and in agony,
> Up-starting from the fiendish crowd
> Of shapes and thoughts that tortured me: . . .
> For all seemed guilt, remorse or woe,
> My own or others still the same
> Life-stifling fear, soul-stifling shame.

> So two nights passed: the night's dismay
> Saddened and stunned the coming day.
> Sleep, the wide blessing, seemed to me
> Distemper's worst calamity.

(P 389-90)

The dream here is obviously something horrific, rather than creative, and in this poem of 1803 Coleridge is clearly beginning to relate his own experience to that of the fictional Mariner, written five years before.

This suggests the sort of significance which he eventually assigned to the dream, both as a literary and a psychological phenomenon. It was a path into the deep levels of the unconscious mind, quite distinct from the shallow half-waking 'reverie' or day-dream. It was a transformation of reality, 'charged' with meanings that might take years to reveal themselves on the mundane, conscious level. (In this sense the Coleridgean dream is opposed to reverie in exactly the same way that imagination is opposed to fancy, or symbol to allegory.) It is a mode of reconciliation between time and eternity, which Coleridge was even inclined to believe might take the form of 'divination', shadowing forth of future events, as he explains in the *Statesman's Manual*. For such dreams are

> ... States, of which it would be scarcely too bold to say that we *dream the things themselves*; so exact, minute, and vivid beyond all power of ordinary memory is the portraiture, so marvellously perfect is our brief metempsychosis into the very *being*, as it were, of the person who seems to address us. ... Not only may we expect, that men of strong religious feelings, but little religious knowledge, will occasionally be tempted to regard such occurrences as supernatural visitations; but it ought not to surprise us, if such dreams should sometimes be confirmed by the event, as though they had actually possessed a character of divination. For ... who shall determine, to what extent this reproductive imagination, unsophisticated by the will, and undistracted by intrusions from the senses, may or may not be concentred and sublimed into foresight and presentment? (LS 80-1)

Coleridge presents this possibility only as a speculation; but it is characteristic of him to believe that the mind, 'unsophisticated by the will', has unfathomable powers. He goes on to suggest that the curious relations of dream time to everyday time might lead one to suppose that there was some undeveloped 'inner sense' in our natures which 'stood to the relations of Time as the power of gravitation to those of Space'. The dream imagination, like the artistic imagination, might somehow be capable of 'enchanting' objects from out of their temporal sphere, as 'for instance, the gravity in the sun and the moon' can hold sway over 'the spring tides of our ocean' (LS 82).

Thus one dream, or one poem, drawn from the very depth of the unconscious mind, might mysteriously hold sway over the tides of one man's entire life, and be a symbol of its permanent meaning.

3 The Mariner

> Argument: How a Ship, having first sailed to the Equator, was driven by Storms to the cold Country towards the South Pole; how the Ancient Mariner cruelly and in contempt of the laws of hospitality killed a Sea-bird and how he was followed by many and strange Judgements: and in what manner he came back to his own Country. (P 186)

The idea that *The Rime of the Ancient Mariner* (P 186–209) might turn out to be the story of Coleridge's whole life first came to Coleridge himself during the voyage to Malta in 1804. It has attracted biographers ever since, despite the obvious inconvenience that the poem was first written (though not completed) when Coleridge was only twenty-six, and could hardly know what his life held in store. Certainly, interpreted in any literal fashion it leads quickly to the absurdities of the Ken Russell psycho-biographic film, made in 1977, in which the Albatross turns out to be Mrs Coleridge draped round the poet's neck in a small rowing boat rocking perilously on Derwent Water.

Yet could the poem be a 'dream' of his life, in the sense we have been examining? Or, to put it another way, could the *Mariner* bear a symbolic relationship to his work as a whole, expressing the spiritual journey towards transcendent truth which his *Biographia* proclaims and his entire career, with its many sufferings and 'strange Judgements', seems to witness?

The *Mariner* has been subjected to more interpretations than any other part of Coleridge's work, though as in the case of 'Kubla Khan' these have generally been based on logical schemas applied from outside, rather than treating the poem as an organic whole, based on those 'self-circling energies of the Reason' which gave birth 'to a system of symbols, harmonious in themselves'.

These schemas have tended to be broadly of three kinds. The first is biographical, in which the Mariner is Coleridge, the Albatross is one of his loved ones (alternatively Sara Coleridge, Sara Hutchinson, or even Dorothy Wordsworth), and the Mariner's sufferings are expressive of Coleridge's opium addiction, and moral collapse, which is eventually cured by his return to the 'harbour' of his work and friendships.

The second interpretation is religious or sacramental. Here the killing of the Albatross is a sin against God or nature, the Mariner's sufferings are a form of purgatorial fire, and his return to harbour, with the ministrations of the old Hermit, represents salvation and acceptance into the divine community of the 'kirk', with its Christian 'wedding feast'. The third approach may be called aesthetic: the Mariner is seen as a forerunner of the *poète maudit*, the artist who breaks the bounds of convention in his search for beauty and self-knowledge, passes through a terrible time of trial, and is eventually saved by the powers of a Coleridgean imagination (watching the beautiful sea beasts), though condemned to re-tell his tale to a largely uncomprehending audience (the Wedding Guest) ever after.

Each of these interpretations has its attractions, and all three reflect the recognition of a tripartite movement in the poem – the journey out, the trial and revelation, the journey back – which has an obvious bearing on Coleridge's life. This movement also recalls one of the oldest forms of European romance-tale, the *rite de passage*, as found for example in the Arthurian legends, and the Middle English Christian-chivalric romance, *Sir Gawain and the Green Knight*. Indeed the Mariner in his ship, and Sir Gawain on his horse, go through oddly parallel adventures (both related at a time of ritual feasting).

However, each fresh return to the poem somehow has the effect of throwing off these sophisticated literary readings. Each time, what strikes the reader is the primitive, naked, literal quality of the ballad: its bright, glaring statement of events, and its rough-cut, sea-shanty rhymes:

> 'The ship was cheered, the harbour cleared,
> Merrily did we drop
> Below the kirk, below the hill,
> Below the lighthouse top.
>
> The Sun came up upon the left,
> Out of the sea came he!
> And he shone bright, and on the right
> Went down into the sea.'

It carries the conviction of a child's painting: the sharp, clear shapes and colours, the flat bold two-dimensional movements – the ship 'dropping' below the hill, the sun sliding up 'out of' the sea, like cut-outs. (Later the poet will confirm this first impression, with his description 'As idle as a painted ship / Upon a painted ocean'.) Behind it too, in the rhythms, seems to play some hypnotic folk tune, or nursery rhyme, with suggestions of hands clapping, elbows jerking in time, a fiddle playing perhaps, or a tin whistle, or a child's drum. It is simple, 'merry', even faintly *silly*: yet behind it lies something else, something larger and just slightly menacing, which we have already caught in the 'glittering' eye of the Mariner, as he 'stoppeth' one of the three wedding guests to tell his tale. One notices too the curious effect of that exclamation mark: as if the sun, as if 'he', came out of the sea with more than usual power; or as if the sea itself released the sun that day with more than usual deliberation and intent; – and perhaps – the thought hovers on the edge of that exclamation – with conscious malice: 'Out of the sea came he!' *Beware*!

Such initial impressions are vital to the truth of the poem. They insist that the *Mariner* is, first and foremost, about what it says it is: a primitive tale of a sailor and the sea, told with absolute directness, where the elements and celestial bodies play their parts like people – Sun, Moon, Sea, Stars, Wind, Storm – and nature and supernature easily overlap. Moreover the directness of the verse has nothing to do with 'realism', any more than a child's painting, or the Bayeux tapestry, or an animated cartoon is realistic. It is on the contrary highly stylised, making ingenious use of the ballad conventions, and depending for its power on a number of formal qualities, associated with the flat, two-dimensional brightness of the poem.

The first is the emphasis on spatial movement: physical movements of speed and stillness, rising, falling, hovering and hanging, circling and centring, changing to new geographical and navigational positions; and then metaphysical movements, crossing the boundaries between zones, fields of influence, levels of awareness, frames of reference, natural and supernatural frontiers, sacred and profane hemispheres. One can express this, for a moment, diagrammatically, by imagining a matchstick ship resting on the line of the sea, the mast in the air, the keel below the surface. Everything that happens in the poem belongs to one of the three zones thus demarcated: either in the sky, on the surface, or below in the invisible depths. Each zone contains the things proper to its element, and each crossing or trespassing between the zones may be propitious, dangerous, evil, or perhaps redemptory.

The second formal quality is that of light and colour. Both the sun and the moon bring with them special symbolic effects of weather and luminosity. The sun is frequently red, menacing, parching, burning, purgatorial and cruel. The moon meanwhile is white, glimmering, cool, magical, healing. Various elements move between these two extremes, often with sudden bursts of lurid radiance, presaging strange events: 'And ice, mast high, came floating by, / As green as emerald', or with slow, melting, transpositions of tone, which are often used to lull the reader into false security: '"Whiles all the night, through fog-smoke white, / Glimmered the white Moon-shine."' In the next stanza, the Albatross is shot.

Besides the stylised use of spatial position, and lighting effects, the *Mariner* draws powerfully on the old ballad tradition of using supernatural events, spirits and visions as if they were the norm of human experience, and not to be sharply distinguished in the story from everyday natural agencies and forces. The ship may be driven equally by a spirit, or a storm blast; the sun may be obscured equally by a low black cloud, or a spectral vessel. This deliberate use of supernatural phenomena is one of the most disturbing to modern readers, who instinctively tend towards a psychological and subjective interpretation of such 'imagery', finding it difficult to accept that the spirits are carefully placed, out there in the narrative, as objective identities, who are far more active in the unfolding of the journey than the Mariner himself. After his single act of shooting of the Albatross he is an almost entirely passive spectator, or sufferer, of events. The supernatural world, by contrast, is increasingly violent and masterful in its deeds, at first gaining control of the ship; then possessing the dead bodies of the entire crew (except for the Mariner); and finally, after driving the ship at preternatural speeds back to its proper hemisphere and harbour, sinking it like lead.

Coleridge placed, as an epigraph to the poem, a Latin passage from Thomas Burnet's *Archaeologiae Philosophicae*, not on the subject of sea voyages, but on the problems posed by the existence of invisible spirits, their powers and natures: *Facile credo, plures esse Naturas invisibiles quam visibiles* . . . (P 186). ('I can easily believe that there are more invisible than visible Beings in the Universe. But who will explain to us the kind and family of each? And their order of rank, relationships, distinguishing qualities, and special functions? What it is they do? In what places do they dwell? For the human Mind always circles around these things, but never attains knowledge of them. . . . ') This journey into the world of the 'invisible Beings', the *terra incognita* about which the mind circles restlessly, is clearly the heart of the Mariner's experience, and forms the main narrative structure of the ballad.

In Part I, the Mariner relates how his ship, having passed the Equator in good weather, is driven far into the southern seas of ice and snow by a 'Storm-blast', which struck them 'with his o'ertaking wings'. They are enclosed by ice which 'cracked and growled, and roared and howled', like some unseen beast, and remain trapped until the appearance of the Albatross which the crew hail 'As if it had been a Christian soul'. Up to the point when the Mariner shoots the Albatross (Part I, final stanza), all these phenomena appear essentially natural, though the hints of 'unknown modes of Being' (in the Wordsworthian phrase) are strong in the language of the ballad and its personifications.

In Part II, the ship is blown back to the line of the Equator in the Pacific. 'We were the first that ever burst / Into that silent sea.' Here they are becalmed under the burning sun, and the crew begins to suffer the terrible pangs of drought. The boards of the ship shrink, and the sailors undergo hallucinations. They are now on the very borders of the visible and the invisible, the natural and the supernatural. For the first time, a Spirit enters the narrative: 'Nine fathom deep he had followed us / From the land of mist and snow.'

The Spirit of the deep first enters the world of the sailors through their dreams or unconscious mind: and a powerful correlation is thus set up between that which is physically and that which is mentally hidden, 'in the depths'. Throughout the rest of the *Mariner*, the ocean and the mind are in 'correspondence', or symbolic relationship. The sailors now hang the corpse of the Albatross round the Mariner's neck: a first ritual gesture, which signifies both the recognition of guilt – and an attempt to escape its consequences. Whatever the Albatross may or may not have stood for in the beginning, the crew have now invested it with symbolic importance, and it too moves across the line dividing the visible from the invisible world. It becomes 'charged'.

In Part III, the sailors are approaching the point of total collapse and death. The whole section is presented through a filter of red, with images of low burning sunset light, and blood sucked from the vein or dripping from the heart. The spirit world now directly invades their own, as a ship appears on the western horizon, moving across the face of the sun ('As if through a dungeon-grate he peered') with black ribs and transparent sails. This is the spectre-bark, with its crew of two (Death and the lurid woman Life-in-Death, a sort of parody of the wedding couple), who dice for the lives of the sailors. The deliberate introduction of a cruel element of chance here, with each man's life (or perhaps just the Mariner's?) depending on the fall of the dice, seems a deliberate rejection by Coleridge of any morally ordered universe, and an emphatic confirmation of the objective powers of the spirit world. It also leads to the most obviously 'existential' moment in the ballad, when the Mariner is confronted simultaneously by the horror and indifferent loveliness of the world of nature:

> The Sun's rim dips; the stars rush out:
> At one stride comes the dark;
> With far-heard whisper, o'er the sea,
> Off shot the spectre-bark.
>
> We listened and looked sideways up!
> Fear at my heart, as at a cup,
> My life-blood seemed to sip!
> The stars were dim, and thick the night,
> The steersman's face by his lamp gleamed white;
> From the sails the dew did drip –
> Till clomb above the eastern bar

> The hornéd Moon, with one bright star
> Within the nether tip.

It is one of the passages which Coleridge kept adding to, and adjusting, until the edition of 1817. The sinister beauty of the word 'stride'; the physically repellent but undoubtedly sacramental image of fear sipping from the heart 'as at a cup'; the unearthly calm of the dripping dew; the determination and grimness of the steersman's white face; the remoteness of the 'one bright star' *within* the Moon's horn (a sailor's omen of bad luck) – all these are master combinations of hope and utter despair. Immediately after this, the rest of the crew – 'four times fifty living men' – drop down lifeless, and the Mariner is left finally alone.

Part IV of the ballad is the crisis of the Mariner's experience. 'Alone, alone, all, all alone, / Alone on a wide wide sea!', for seven days and nights he is hypnotised by the 'curse' in his dead comrades' eyes. His heart is 'dry as dust' and he cannot pray. The moon's beams 'mock the sultry bay', and he gazes up at her 'yearning' for a spiritual home as in the beautiful prose gloss which Coleridge wrote in 1814. Then follows the moment when the Mariner turns back to the sea, and in silent wonder watches the serpents playing on the surface: they are shining white in the path of the moon, and in the shadow of the ship 'Blue, glossy green, and velvet black'. At last comes that central, primordial act of 'blessing' – a movement of the whole heart and mind, without words or gesture – which confirms them in their beauty, their otherness, their right to be alive, their right to have place and home and existence in the universe:

> O happy living things! no tongue
> Their beauty might declare:
> A spring of love gushed from my heart,
> And I blessed them unaware:
> Sure my kind saint took pity on me,
> And I blessed them unaware.

The repetition of 'unaware' is curiously striking, since so much of the ballad seems to concern precisely the growth of the Mariner's awareness of what he has done. The effect is to make his act of blessing utterly innocent, utterly spontaneous. It comes, as we say, 'straight from the heart'. It is in fact the proof of his true nature; yet it is as mysterious in its origins as his act of shooting the Albatross. In the language of the theologian, it is an 'act of Grace', apparently independent of the conscious human will, yet in accord with the divine. The words of Paul Tillich, in *The Shaking of the Foundations* (1949), have perhaps some bearing here, where he says that sin is *separation*, and grace a *re-uniting*: 'the *re*union of life with life, the *re*conciliation of the self with itself. Grace is the acceptance of that which is rejected. . . .' In the prose gloss Coleridge writes: 'He blesseth them in his heart. The spell begins to break.' The Albatross drops from the Mariner's neck, and sinks 'Like lead into the sea'. For the first time the Mariner sleeps.

It is just at this point, when some sort of Christian redemptive interpretation seems about to dominate the ballad, that its primitive and magical elements reassert themselves most strongly, and the terror and disorientation of the Mariner increases. In Part V, the Mariner wakes to find the upper air above the ship torn by 'strange sights and commotions', black clouds, great sheets of soundless lightning, and a roaring wind that never seems to reach the sails. The dead crew rise up and man the ship 'beneath the lightning and the Moon', to the horror of the Mariner:

> The body of my brother's son
> Stood by me, knee to knee:
> The body and I pulled at one rope,
> But he said nought to me.

That grim denial of domestic recognition removes all reassurance from this 'troop of spirits blest'; and when the dead men pray together at dawn 'clustered round the mast', the utter exclusion of the Mariner is only emphasised. Moreover the ship is being moved, not by any divine or natural breeze, but from *beneath* by the revenging Polar Spirit 'Under the keel nine fathom deep'. At noon, with the sun right above the mast, the ship halts and begins to tremble, jerking back and forth, and the Mariner collapses on the deck in a swoon. As he lies there, he hears two voices, 'the Polar Spirit's fellow-daemons', discussing his fate. From one he learns that the spirit 'who bideth by himself / In the land of mist and snow' had 'loved the bird that loved the man / Who shot him with his bow.'

Thus the Mariner understands that by cruelly and ignorantly trespassing on the realm of the upper air, and all that signifies, he has broken some invisible circle of love and trust ('the laws of hospitality') of which he unwittingly formed part: as a result he has excited the vengeance of a spirit of the lower sphere. Moreover, as the second voice says, ('As soft as honey-dew'): he has done penance, but 'penance more will do'.

In Part VI, the Mariner recovers consciousness to find the ship sailing in the calm night beneath the moon; but now the entire crew are standing together on the deck with eyes fixed on him. This collective gaze of communal accusation is the most horrific thing the Mariner has to confront: though unnatural – because they are dead – it is also completely human. (What resonances does it stir in the modern reader – what groups of 'undead' men standing with glittering, accusing eyes beneath towers, behind barbed wire, in compounds, in courtyards, behind bolts and bars?)

> All stood together on the deck,
> For a charnel-dungeon fitter:
> All fixed on me their stony eyes
> That in the Moon did glitter.
>
> The pang, the curse, with which they died,
> Had never passed away:
> I could not draw my eyes from theirs,
> Nor turn them up to pray.

No action of the Mariner can redeem this: indeed the sufferings of the crew have been irredeemable. The image of the 'frightful fiend' that pursues him on a 'lonesome road' suggests that the Mariner's guilt will have to be expiated endlessly, until journey's end, which is life's. Coleridge merely says that after an unspecified time 'this spell was snapt', and the Mariner finds himself to his wonder and disbelief, sailing into his own harbou` 'Is this the hill? Is this the kirk? / Is this mine own countree? The realisation is abrupt, and deliberately dream-like, the water 'clear as glass' and the familiar landscape suffused in moonlight. It is almost as if he had never left. Behind him he sees the crew's bodies now lying peacefully on the deck, each one guarded by a 'seraph-man', all light. In front of him he hears the dash of oars, and sees a Pilot Boat carrying the old Hermit towards the ship. The Mariner's thoughts immediately turn to his own guilt: 'He'll shrieve my soul, he'll wash away / The Albatross's blood.'

The final section of the ballad, Part VII, opens with the Mariner listening to the voices in the approaching Pilot Boat – at first cheerful, then puzzled, then alarmed, as they realise the condition of the ship: '"Dear Lord! it hath a fiendish look –".' The roles are curiously reversed as the Mariner discovers that for these ordinary mortals it is now *he* who is on a 'spectre-bark'. A moment later a dreadful rumbling is heard beneath the water, as if the Polar Spirit has pursued the Mariner into the very safety of the harbour, and with a sound that 'split the bay' the ship instantly founders.

The Mariner's final return into human hands is cunningly managed so as to emphasise his total disorientation. Has he been hallucinating, has he been dreaming, or has he been really dead?

> Like one that hath been seven days drowned
> My body lay afloat;
> But swift as dreams, myself I found
> Within the Pilot's boat.

The Mariner begs the holy man to shrive him, and only then does he begin to understand the nature of his penance:

> Forthwith this frame of mine was wrenched
> With a woeful agony,
> Which forced me to begin my tale;
> And then it left me free.

> Since then, at an uncertain hour,
> That agony returns:
> And till my ghastly tale is told,
> This heart within me burns.

I pass, like night, from land to land,
I have strange power of speech;
That moment that his face I see,
I know the man that must hear me:
To him my tale I teach.

Thus the Mariner becomes the traditional figure of the Wandering Jew, as Coleridge indicated in his notebooks, who 'had told this story ten thousand times since' (N I No. 45, Notes). Yet not the traditional figure at all, because his experiences, while making him an outcast from society, have also given him a permanent role and duty within the human community. To make other people share everything he has undergone and learned through suffering. His tale to *teach*, by a constantly repeated act of the imagination. This aspect is carefully confirmed in the prose gloss: 'And to teach, by his own example, love and reverence to all things that God made and loveth.'

In the closing stanzas of the ballad, Coleridge brings back the sounds and jollity of the wedding feast, allowing the Mariner to emphasise his love for his fellow men – the kirk and the 'goodly company', and a humble affirmation of the 'one Life': 'He prayeth well, who loveth well / Both man and bird and beast.' The pious naïveté of this, which seems to bear little relation to the existential horror of the Mariner's experiences, is deliberate: a skilful use of the ballad convention of the 'moral', which leaves the same kind of sense of things unsaid, vast forces felt but not fully acknowledged, as has been established in Part I. Something of this is recognised in the reaction of the Wedding Guest: 'He went like one that hath been stunned, / And is of sense forlorn.'

The figure of the Wedding Guest in fact plays a vital role throughout the ballad – his voice appears at critical moments both in Part III and Part IV (including the disturbing couplet provided by Wordsworth, comparing the Mariner to the long, lank, brown expanse of 'the ribbed sea-sand') – and it is to him that the Mariner makes the chilling remark that undercuts the whole tone of the ballad's conclusion:

O Wedding-Guest! this soul hath been
Alone on a wide wide sea:

> So lonely 'twas, that God himself
> Scarce seemed there to be.

This seems to be unmistakably and unavoidably the voice of Coleridge: of Coleridge at Nether Stowey, at Keswick, at Malta, at the Greyhound Inn, Bath, and probably at moments walking in the evening garden at Highgate. Chronology is immaterial here, for it is a note that, once struck in someone's life, will resound again and again 'at an uncertain hour'. Moreover it is a note unheard of elsewhere in English poetry at the time: Wordsworth, we know, did not understand it; Shelley would not have credited it; Byron would have regarded it as unpardonable bad form. It is a note that, as with so much of Coleridge, we have to turn to Europe to hear repeated: in Friedrich Hölderlin perhaps, who went mad; or Gérard de Nerval who committed suicide. In England we do not really hear it again, except for dark moments in Tennyson and Hardy, until the poetry of the First World War, with its terrible pity and simplicity.

If the journey of the *Mariner* recounts a descent into hell, *une saison en enfer*, a voyage into a condition where God himself scarce seemed to be, it also recounts a return. The whole dualism of the poem – the sun and the moon, the powers of water and air, the act of killing and the act of blessing, the state of solitude and the state of 'goodly company', the nightmare and the awakening, the drowning and the resurfacing – all suggests that some kind of redemption or reconciliation is possible. Yet the terms of this reconciliation are not there in the ballad. It remains obstinately, brilliantly, a 'self-circling' system of energies and symbols, in which even the Mariner's own attempt to impose a Christian meaning and value on everything that has happened is spun away into the endless repetition of his story: 'I know the man that must hear me: / To him my tale I teach.' After such knowledge, what forgiveness?

Coleridge the writer, the thinker and teacher, may not be in any equivalent sense Coleridge the Mariner. Yet I am much mistaken if, even now, we do not hear his story and listen to what he says, like so many Wedding Guests:

> 'By thy long grey beard and glittering eye,
> Now wherefore stopp'st thou *me*?'

Further reading

The place of publication is London unless otherwise indicated.

Coleridge's works

The most useful and inspiring selection is the Penguin *Portable Coleridge*, edited by I. A. Richards (Harmondsworth, 1978), which includes all the major poetry, and a good choice from the letters, the notebooks, the *Biographia*, *The Friend*, and various lectures. The standard edition of the poetry is *Coleridge: Poetical Works*, edited by E. H. Coleridge (Oxford, 1912, repr. 1980; also in paperback). Convenient editions of some of the prose can be found in Dent's Everyman's Library: *Biographia Literaria*, edited by G. Watson (1965), and *Shakespearean Criticism*, edited by T. M. Raysor (2 vols., 1960). The correspondence is published in *Collected Letters of Samuel Taylor Coleridge*, edited by E. L. Griggs (6 vols., Oxford, 1956–71). Enormously valuable are *The Notebooks of Samuel Taylor Coleridge*, edited by Kathleen Coburn (3 vols., 1794–1819, each volume consisting of two parts, text and notes; Routledge, 1957–); and see also *Inquiring Spirit*, edited by K. Coburn (1951).

For the rest, the problem is finding good editions of the prose. The *Biographia Literaria*, edited by J. Shawcross (2 vols., Oxford, 1907), includes additional essays not available in the Everyman edition, and excellent notes. Useful Victorian editions are *The Complete Works of Samuel Taylor Coleridge*, edited by W. G. T. Shedd (7 vols., New York, 1884); the Bohn Library *Aids to Reflection*, edited by H. N. Coleridge (1884); or the Morley's Universal Library *Table Talk*, edited by H. Morley (1884). A new Bollingen Series edition of *The Collected Works of Samuel Taylor Coleridge*, scholarly, magnificent and expensive, is being produced under the general editorship of K. Coburn (Princeton University Press and Routledge). Especially valuable, of the volumes published thus far, are: 1, *Lectures 1795 on Politics and Religion*, edited by L. Patton and P. Mann (1971); 3, *Essays on His Times*, edited by D. V. Erdman (3 vols., 1978), which contains all Coleridge's occasional journalism; 4, *The Friend*, edited by B. E. Rooke (2 vols., 1969); 6, *Lay Sermons*, edited by R. J. White (1972); 10, *On the Constitution of the Church and State*, edited by J. Colmer (1976).

Works on Coleridge

The best introductory studies are: *Coleridge* by Humphrey House (1953); *Coleridge* by Walter Jackson Bate (1968); *Coleridge* by M. Bernard Delvaille (Paris, 1967); and *A Preface to Coleridge* by Allan Grant, which gives documentary background and illustrations (1972). An excellent critical survey of all aspects, including the poetry, plays, political journalism, philosophy, etc. is *Coleridge* by Katharine Cooke (1979).

On the biographical side, no one should miss William Hazlitt's 'On My First Acquaintance with Poets' (1823) and 'Mr Coleridge' in *The Spirit of the Age* (1825). The standard life is still *Samuel Taylor Coleridge* by E. K. Chambers (1938), which is finely detailed, but unsympathetic about the work. *Coleridge and Sara Hutchinson and the Asra Poems* by George Whalley (1955) opens up the poet's emotional life. *Wordsworth and Coleridge* by H. M. Margoliouth (1953) is solid and brief. *Coleridge: Poet and Revolutionary, 1772–1804* by John Cornwell (1973) is an excellent critical biography, though incomplete. A full-scale treatment of the poet–addict theme is sensitively managed in *Samuel Taylor Coleridge: A Bondage of Opium* by Molly Lefebure (1974).

J. S. Mill's fine essay on Coleridge is reprinted in *Mill on Bentham and Coleridge*, edited by F. R. Leavis (1950); this should be followed up with *Culture and Society 1780–1950* by Raymond Williams (Pelican edn., Harmondsworth, 1961). Very useful groundwork on Coleridge's thought is also provided by *Edmund Burke and the Revolt against the Eighteenth Century* by Alfred Cobban (1929). More detailed studies can be found in *Coleridge, Critic of Society* by John Colmer (1959); *Coleridge and the Idea of the Modern State* by D. P. Calleo (1966). The philosophical and religious development is traced out in *What Coleridge Thought* by Owen Barfield (Middletown, Conn., 1972); *Coleridge the Visionary* by John Beer (1959); *Coleridge and the Idea of Love* by A. J. Harding (Cambridge, 1974); *Coleridge and Christian Doctrine* by J. R. Barth (Cambridge, Mass., 1969); and a brilliant, difficult work which tries to reconcile all these aspects, *Coleridge and the Pantheist Tradition* by Thomas McFarland (1969).

Valuable and often amusing background is provided by *Coleridge*, edited by J. R. de J. Jackson (1970), in Routledge's The Critical Heritage series, which reprints contemporary reviews and essays 1794–1834. *The Road to Xanadu* by J. Livingstone Lowes (Paladin edn., 1980) is a classic study of Coleridgean sources. A clear, comprehensive account of the poetry is *The Waking Dream* by Patricia Adair (1967). More subtle and advanced studies are *Coleridge and Wordsworth: the Poetry of Growth* by Stephen Prickett (Cambridge, 1970), and *Coleridge and the Abyssi-*

man Maid by Geoffrey Yarlott (1967). For the criticism, *Coleridge on Imagination* by I. A. Richards (1934) is still excellent; after which the reader may like to move on to *Method and Imagination in Coleridge's Criticism* by J. R. de J. Jackson (1969); and *The Idea of Coleridge's Criticism* by R. H. Fogle (1962). On poetic and religious symbolism, see *The Starlit Dome* by G. Wilson Knight (1959); *Further Explorations* by L. C. Knights (1965); and *The Idea of the Symbol* by M. Jadwiga Swiatecka O. P. (Cambridge, 1980). On the *Mariner*, the essay, 'A Poem of Pure Imagination', in *Selected Essays* by Robert Penn Warren (1964) is indispensable.

The development of the plagiarism controversy can be followed from *Recollections of the Lakes and the Lake Poets* by Thomas De Quincey (Penguin edn., Harmondsworth, 1970), and 'The Plagiarisms of S. T. Coleridge' by J. C. Ferrier in *Blackwood's Magazine*, vol. XLVII (March 1840). From there the reader should go to the editorial notes of T. M. Raysor in *Shakespearean Criticism*, and J. Shawcross in *Biographia Literaria*, in the editions cited above, and the detailed study *The Indebtedness of S. T. Coleridge to A. W. Schlegel* by A. A von Helmholtz (1907). A general and rather hostile account is provided by René Wellek in *A History of Modern Criticism*, vol. I (1955); but see also the studies by Thomas McFarland and Molly Lefebure cited above. The whole position, both literary and psychological, has been explored at length in *Coleridge, the Damaged Archangel* by Norman Fruman (1972), which though antagonistic yields some brilliant insights into Coleridge's struggles.

On the European context, see two essays by Herbert Read, 'The Notion of Organic Form' and 'Coleridge as Critic', in his *The True Voice of Feeling* (1968), and for readers of French, *La Formation de la pensée de Coleridge* by M. Paul Deschamps (Paris, 1964), and *Coleridge et Schelling* by Gabriel Marcel (Paris, 1971). More demanding is *Coleridge and German Idealism* by George Orsini (1969). The philosophical background is authoritatively set out by René Wellek in *Immanuel Kant in England* (1950). Extremely original and sympathetic is *The Dark Night of Samuel Taylor Coleridge* by Marshall Suther (1960), which ends with a general chapter on the 'Romantic Échec' in European poetry.

Index